Voices of Dissent

INQUIRY INTO CRUCIAL AMERICAN PROBLEMS

Series Editor · JACK R. FRAENKEL

Voices of Dissent:

Positive Good or Disruptive Evil?

FRANK KANE

Department Chairman, Social Studies
Jefferson High School
Daly City, California

PRENTICE-HALL, INC.   ENGLEWOOD CLIFFS, N.J.

Titles in this series:

© Copyright 1970 by Prentice-Hall, Inc.,
Englewood Cliffs, N.J.
All rights reserved. No part
of this book may be
reproduced in any form
or by any means
without permission
in writing from the publisher.

Printed in the United States of America

13-943613-8 paper
13-943621-9 cloth

1 2 3 4 5 6 7 8 9 10

Prentice-Hall International, Inc.,
London
Prentice-Hall of Australia, Pty. Ltd.,
Sydney
Prentice-Hall of Canada, Ltd.,
Toronto
Prentice-Hall of India Private Ltd.,
New Delhi
Prentice-Hall of Japan, Inc.,
Tokyo

PREFACE

The series *INQUIRY INTO CRUCIAL AMERICAN PROB-LEMS* focuses upon a number of important contemporary social and political issues. Each book presents an in-depth study of a particular problem, selected because of its pressing intrusion into the minds and consciences of most Americans today. A major concern has been the desire to make the materials relevant to students. Every title in the series, therefore, has been selected because, in one way or another, it suggests a problem of concern to students today.

A number of divergent viewpoints, from a wide variety of different *kinds* of sources, encourage discussion and reflection and illustrate that the same problem may be viewed from many different vantage points. Of concern throughout is a desire to help students realize that honest men may legitimately differ in their views.

After a short chapter introducing the questions with which the book will deal, Chapter 2 presents a brief historical and contemporary background so that students will have more than just a superficial understanding of the problem under study. In the readings that follow, a conscientious effort has been made to avoid endorsing any one viewpoint as the "right" viewpoint, or to evaluate the arguments of particular individuals. No conclusions are drawn. Instead, a number of questions for discussion and reflection are posed at the end of each reading so that students can come to their own conclusions.

Great care has been taken to insure that the readings included in each book are just that—readable! We have searched particularly for articles that are of high interest, yet from which differing viewpoints may be legitimately inferred. Whenever possible, dialogues involving or descriptions showing actual people responding and reacting to problematic situations are presented. In sum, each book

- presents divergent, conflicting views on the problem under consideration;

- gives as many perspectives and dimensions on the problem as space permits;

- presents articles on a variety of reading levels, in order to appeal to students of many different ability levels;

- presents analytical as well as descriptive statements;

- deals with real people involved in situations of concern to them;

- includes questions which encourage discussion and thought of the various viewpoints expressed;

- includes activities to involve students to consider further the issues embedded in the problem.

CONTENTS

Introduction

In a West Virginia schoolhouse, the teacher calls the class to attention, asks the students to stand for the salute to the flag, and at once notices that several of the students have remained seated. They are members of Jehovah's Witnesses, a religious group that considers the salute in violation of its religious beliefs. The students who refused to salute are expelled from school and are threatened with being put into a reformatory for the "criminally inclined." The Witnesses fight the decision in the courts. Eventually the Supreme Court of the United States upholds their right to remain silent when the "pledge" is being said.

In San Francisco, a group of hippies walks naked in the panhandle of Golden Gate Park. They are demonstrating their contempt for the middle-class ethic that associates nudity with shamefulness. The hippies are arrested by the police, and are carted off to jail.

In a midwestern town, on Christmas Eve, a young man parades before the local draft board in a protest against military conscription. At midnight, in freezing temperatures, he barely manages to light a candle with his burning draft card. He goes to jail for the fourth time.

In Montgomery, Alabama, Negro citizens, under the leadership of the late Dr. Martin Luther King, decide that they have had enough of separate "colored" sections in the back of public buses. They stage a boycott, without violence, and walk miles rather than board a bus. There are no more segregated buses in Montgomery.

In a small town in New England, a husband and wife appear before a special meeting of the Board of Trustees of the school district. They are protesting the principal's rule that prevents their seventeen-year-old daughter from returning to school. Just previous to her senior year the girl had given birth to an illegitimate child, had sent the infant to an adoption agency, and now wishes to complete her schooling. On the grounds that the girl's presence would constitute a "moral hazard" to the other students, the Board upholds the principal.

In several Western states, members of the Native American Church (an American Indian religious group) smoke peyote in connection with certain ceremonial rites. In one state, they are held in violation of the state narcotics law. The Indians appeal to the courts, and their right to use this hallucinatory drug is upheld by the State Supreme Court.

In Miami Beach, Florida, a group of atheists is refused radio time for a program to expound its ideas. The atheists appeal to the Federal Communications Commission, but are turned down because such a program would "offend the conscience of a Christian nation."

In San Francisco, a teacher at San Francisco City College refuses to answer questions to the House Un-American Activities Committee concerning his membership in the Communist Party during the 1940's. The Board of Trustees dismisses him from his job at the college. He appeals through the courts, and about ten years later receives $136,000 in back pay, plus reinstatement in his job.

In Chicago, a woman who works as a teller in a major bank receives less pay than the man at the next window for doing the same work. She brings suit against the bank, charging discrimination on the basis of sex, wins the case, and receives back pay as well as an increase in salary.

In Columbus, Ohio, a group of American Nazis request the use of a high school auditorium for a public meeting. The purpose of the meeting is to explain their views on the racial crisis. The Board of Trustees turns them down on the ground that a public school "should not be a forum for purveyors of hate."

In the city of Los Angeles, hundreds of citizens of Spanish surname parade before voter registration tables at stores and other public places. The signs they carry all bear a similar message to one saying "California voting laws discriminate against Mexican Americans." This is a protest against the state law which requires that a person must read and write the English language before he may vote. A few members of the legislature react, but nothing is done.

It is evident, of course, that there is something similar in all these cases. These are people who are involved in one way or another in dissent or protest. They are generally individuals or groups with strong convictions, and for that reason are often willing to take the long hard road to correct what they consider to be unjust or discriminatory or morally wrong. They may appeal to the Federal or State Constitution; they may appeal to reason; or, as in the case of the bus boycott, they may take direct action. In any case, dissent means disagreement with the way things are; often it is an effort to change things to the way the dissenter feels they ought to be.

Some dissent involves civil rights and civil liberties: people protest against what they feel to be a denial of their full participation in the benefits of our democracy. In other cases, dissenters protest against the existing laws of the land, or the structures of society that no longer seem relevant.

The constant flood of protestors and dissenters helps to fill our courtrooms and other judicial agencies—not to mention our jails. Are people unaware of what they may or may not do without being punished? Might they even desire punishment to publicize their aims? Will punishment stop dissent? Should we even try to stop it? To limit it? Or is it a positive force in our society?

The readings that follow may not give you an answer to these questions, but perhaps they will encourage you to think about some of the controversial problems that this country has faced—and is facing today. As you read the individual selections, keep the following questions in mind:

1. What is the motive for the dissent or protest?
2. Why is the dissenter often branded as a "radical"?
3. Is dissent equivalent to disloyalty if the national interest is involved?
4. Does dissent become treason in time of war?
5. Is the nonconformist as rigid in his nonconformity as the person he labels a "conformist"?
6. How far should personal freedom extend? At what point does it conflict with the interests of society?

Is Dissent
Something New?

- Do you usually go along with the group?
- Do you accept a certain amount of injustice as "part of the game"?
- Do you think that it is useless to oppose the established order?
- To what extent would you sacrifice your job, your reputation, or your personal safety to fight against injustice, falsehood, or hypocrisy?
- Are you a dissenter?

This word "dissent" came into English from the Latin, being a combination of the prefix "dis," meaning against or apart, and the verb "sentire," meaning to feel. Thus, the dissenter is the person who is in disagreement with established opinion or practice. He feels apart from the way things are and would like to see a change. Since his ideas are often unpopular with the majority of people, the dissenter is frequently tagged with labels that tend to separate him from the rest of society: he is a "fanatic," an "extremist," a "disturber," or sometimes, simply, a "nut."

Today, with the world in ferment, a glance at a newspaper on any given day will almost always furnish an example of dissent—by students, by minorities, by politicians, and by many others. Has it always been this way? One historian has given a short but pertinent answer to this question when he wrote: "Freedom of thought has been uncommon in history." To the student of history, nothing is more apparent than the gaps of hundreds of years when no "voices" are heard, when there is only silence. One can only speculate about how different the story of mankind would be if the peasant, the serf, or the slave had been granted the same opportunity as others to record his feelings about the world he lived in.

Why has it been this way? Perhaps a few examples will give us a clue.

In ancient Athens, several hundred years before the birth of Christ, a man by the name of Socrates took the poison hemlock and died rather than change his beliefs. This man was a teacher, unusual for his time in that he did not lecture but rather asked questions. Socrates felt that this method of teaching made a person think for himself and kept the mind free from the conceit of those who profess to know everything. But to the leaders of Athens this questioning became embarrassing, if not dangerous, especially when young people started questioning religious beliefs or the authority of the state. Eventually Socrates was brought to trial for corrupting the youth of Athens and for religious heresy. He could have saved his life by admitting error, but he chose to die rather than abandon his principles.

Later, in medieval Europe, John Huss, a teacher and a priest, spoke and wrote against the corruption and worldliness of the church. He advocated a return to the "poor church" in accordance with the ideals of primitive Christianity. Huss was condemned as a heretic and burned at the stake in 1415. In 1633, Galileo, the scientist, was summoned by the Inquisition to answer charges of heresy. The charges involved the scientist's acceptance of the Copernican system, which held that the earth was not the center of the universe. Galileo was called a heretic for proclaiming this belief and was forced to kneel before a vast assembly and renounce his theory. Legend has it that as he rose from his knees he muttered, *E pur si muove* (nevertheless it does move). Although Galileo was allowed to live out his natural life, death by fire was the commonplace reward of those found guilty of heresy.

In colonial America, in the year 1660, Mary Dyer was hanged in the city of Boston. Previous to that, two of her fellow workers had been hanged by the Puritans. The charge: preaching religious beliefs that were contrary to those of the colony. Mary and her companions were Quakers, also known as the Society of Friends, a group which had "peculiar ideas" that were obnoxious to the leaders of the Puritan society—such as the belief that all men and women are equal before God, and that slavery is evil, as are war and capital punishment. It is highly ironical that the Puritans, who came to America seeking religious freedom, were so intolerant themselves.

From these examples it can be seen that in earlier times it was not exactly healthy to oppose the authority of the state and church, or to question the "wisdom" of the past or long-held customs. Dissent threatened the structure of these societies, and so dissent was stamped out as an evil. When does the picture change, and how much does it change?

Historians call the 18th Century the "Age of Enlightenment" because this was a time when men awakened to the idea that reason, rather than tradition or authority, should be the guide in the struggle to improve human society. Up to this period, most of the people in power thought that it was perfectly natural to have different laws for different classes of people, to use torture to get confessions, to put heretics to death, or to tax people to support the established church. Then, in the second half of the 18th Century, men like François Marie Arouet Voltaire emerged, determined to fight against superstition and tyranny. He was twice exiled from Paris for his efforts, and was once sent to the Bastille for writing satire about prominent people. But Voltaire was not executed for his dissent, dying a natural death in 1778.

There were others whose dissent with the established order appeared in books and pamphlets of that period: Jean Jacques Rousseau, John Locke, and Montesquieu, to name a few. As Voltaire survived, so did they, and their writings added to the ever-increasing demand for human liberty, for recognition of the fact that men have "natural rights" which cannot be withheld by kings or other rulers, as well as the demand for keeping the power of government in check if those rights are to be preserved. As it happened, all of these men were Europeans, for the term "Enlightenment" has not been applied directly to America of the 18th Century. But several thousand miles of ocean did not stop the ideas of these men from having an impact on the new world, and colonials of the stature of Thomas Jefferson were familiar with the writings of the "philosophes," as they were called. One document serves as a notable example of the affinity between the Enlightenment and prerevolutionary America.

THE DECLARATION OF INDEPENDENCE

"All men are created equal." What a fantastic notion to a wealthy New England slave trader or a Southern plantation owner of the 1770's! How disturbing even to the mind of an Alexander Hamilton that word "all," a man for whom the word "people" was almost a synonym for "rabble" or "riffraff." And to many others of the time the statement had a dangerous relationship to the word "democracy," which, to them, meant "mobocracy," or rule by the mob. It scarcely needs to be mentioned that to Jefferson it meant that every person is a human being, entitled to equal rights, regardless of status or ability.

There were other ideas in the Declaration of Independence that broke with tradition: the "right" of the people to abolish a government when that government does not respond to the will of the people, or the "duty" of the people to throw out a government when it becomes a despotism. Also important is the right to "life, liberty, and the pursuit of happiness," a phrase apparently borrowed from John Locke, but with one slight change. Property, the final word in Locke's statement, became "pursuit of happiness" in the Declaration, indicating, perhaps, that Jefferson felt that human rights were more important than property rights.

Some critics have tried to downgrade the Declaration by calling it a "bundle of generalities," but the fact remains that to the British of the

18th Century, the document was treason, and sufficient cause for separating a man's body from his head. Regarded as especially treasonous was its condemnation of King George III for violating the natural rights of the colonists in order to establish an "absolute tyranny." True, the Declaration does contain certain general principles and an abstract theory of government, but these are the kind of theories and principles which, if followed, keep a democracy alive. And most certainly to those who have been oppressed by a foreign power or a tyrant at home, Jefferson's call for a "new order" has had the impact of a long lost truth struggling to be set free. How else can one explain the worldwide influence of this document? Over the centuries, its message has been a source of hope and inspiration to countless peoples who have struggled for freedom. Apply to the world today one abstraction inherent in the Declaration—"Man was not made for government, but government was made for man"—and ask, How many of those in seats of power would accept this statement as a "harmless" abstraction?

THE REVOLUTION

As did the Declaration of Independence, Tom Paine's pamphlet "Common Sense" convinced many people that a complete break with England was the only course for the colonists. But how many? Textbooks often give the impression that the Revolution was a popular revolt, with all but a handful of Tories opposed. Actually, this was not the case. Even in England, 19 lords signed a formal protest against the king's decision to make war against the colonies. Two of the highest ranking officers of the king's army and navy refused to serve: Lord Jeffrey Amherst and Admiral Keppel. And throughout the colonies there were thousands who refused to join the Americans in battle against England. Some of these, called Loyalists, fled to Canada or England. Others were tarred and feathered or driven from their homes and places of business. Some were killed. John Adams estimated that even at the height of the Revolution no more than one-third of the colonists were involved in the struggle. As it happens, the rebels won, but it should not be ignored that there was dissent against the dissenters.

THE NEW NATION

There was a lingering fear among many citizens that the men assembled at Philadelphia had created a potential despotism by giving so much power to the central government. The first expression of this fear came in 1794 when a storm of dissent broke out in the West among the farmers of Pennsylvania. Alexander Hamilton, Secretary of the Treasury, seeking an additional source of revenue for the new government, persuaded Congress to impose a tax of 25 per cent on the net price of a gallon of whiskey. To these farmers, or "whiskey boys," as they were called, the tax was oppressive, and they maintained that the federal government did not have the right to impose such a tax. Unable to ship their grain east or south and make a profit, the farmers converted the surplus wheat into whiskey, and this liquor in time became a medium of exchange, much the same as money, which was short in supply in the back country.

Something like a civil war over taxation ensued. When the federal agents went out to collect the taxes, the farmers rioted, tarred and feathered the tax collectors (or any farmer who paid the tax), disrupted the procedure of the federal courts, and beat up federal marshalls. To President Washington, this outbreak was a direct challenge to the supremacy of the central government. From the states he requested, and received, an army of about 12,000 men, and proceeded west in command of the troops. Such a show of force was too much for the "whiskey boys," who took off to the woods. Two were captured and found guilty of high treason, but Washington pardoned them, one because he was a "simpleton," and the other because he was "insane."

The men who wrote the Constitution made no mention of political parties. And, in his Farewell Address, Washington warned against "the baneful effects of the spirit of party," fearing that political opposition would lead to riot or rebellion. His successors in the Federalist party agreed with him, especially when they awakened to the rising popularity of the Republican (also known as Democratic-Republican) party of Jefferson, and the sympathy of that party to France and French democracy. As one historian has noted, "the ties between Jefferson and Jacobin [1] simply confirmed a fundamental Federalist conviction that democracy was a subversive, revolutionary idea."

So, to protect the country from French subversion and native dissent, in 1798 the Congress passed the Alien and Sedition Acts. These laws provided jail terms of up to five years and fines up to $5000 for anyone who wrote or spoke about the President, Congress, or the federal government "with intent to defame them or bring them into contempt or disrepute." In no time at all, 21 Republican newspapermen were jailed, one of whom died from mistreatment while in prison. Matthew Lyon, a Congressman from Vermont who had fought in the Revolutionary War, wrote a letter in the *Vermont Journal* criticizing President John Adams for his "ridiculous pomp" and "selfish avarice." He was arrested and spent four months in a prison with all the accommodations of a medieval dungeon. Mr. Lyon was reelected to Congress while in prison, a clear indication of the turning tide of public opinion.

On a national scale, the resentment against the Federalists came with

---

[1] A political party in France noted for its extremely radical ideas in the cause of liberalism. To a Federalist of the time, calling someone a "Jacobin" was like calling a person a "Communist" today. The association of the Jacobins with the reign of terror led to their downfall.

the election of the Republican party in 1800. The winner, Thomas Jefferson, pardoned all those who had been tried and convicted under the Alien and Sedition laws.

THE ABOLITIONISTS

The most prolonged period of dissent in our early history came in the 1830's with a dispute that divided the nation in bitter quarrel both North and South, and was not finally settled until the end of the Civil War. This discord came about as a result of the activities of the abolitionists, a mixed group of orators, editors, runaway slaves, and free Negroes who demanded an end to slavery and a granting to the Negro of the promises in the Declaration of Independence.

In the beginning years of the movement, toleration for the abolitionists was at a very low level, even in the "free" North. In the City of Brotherly Love (Philadelphia), a mob burned down Pennsylvania Hall, built by the abolitionists to hold protest meetings. Public speeches against slavery were particularly hazardous. Frederick Douglass, a runaway slave turned editor, writer, and speaker, was often greeted by his audience with shouts of derision, with rotten eggs, and even with physical attacks upon his person. Douglass kept on, however, and held firm to the conviction that as long as any one race, sex, or group was denied freedom, no group was safe.

White abolitionists were not spared. In 1837, in Alton, Illinois, a mob tried to stop Elijah P. Lovejoy from printing an antislavery newspaper. Twice they threw his printing press into the river, and when this didn't put a stop to his writing, they murdered him. Another, William Lloyd Garrison, the publisher of the abolitionist newspaper, *The Liberator,* came close to the same fate. In 1835, an angry mob seized him, tied a rope around his neck, and dragged him through the streets of Boston. It was said of Garrison that he "wrote in blood" in his newspaper, but he was no less fervent in his speeches. At Framingham, Massachusetts, he burned a copy of the United States Constitution before several thousand witnesses, calling it "source and parent of all other atrocities—a covenant with death and an agreement with hell." When the slave rebellion led by Nat Turner broke out in Virginia, the South blamed it on Garrison.

Persistence paid off, however, and by 1840 membership in abolition or antislavery societies had grown to over 150,000. Churches that had formerly denied entrance to these "radicals" now accepted them. Most important, abolitionists began to appear in Northern legislatures and Congress. A war was soon to settle the issue behind this dissent.

WOMEN'S RIGHTS

After the Civil War, the scene was again enlivened by the appearance of a dissenter of unusual talents, Victoria Woodhull. She was the first woman to appear before a committee of Congress, and in an age when most women were limited to bearing children or tending the stove, she became Wall Street's first lady stockbroker. At a convention in New York City in 1872, Victoria was nominated for President of the United States on a platform, among other things, of "free love." In a weekly newspaper of her own, she came out for birth control, easier divorce laws, and the right of women to vote. In public speeches Victoria railed against the double standard of morality that applied to men and women, as when the police arrested the prostitute but let the man go free. The suffragettes adopted her for a while, but eventually the movement split over the morality issue—for in the matter of "free love" Miss Woodhull, a very attractive woman, is said to have practiced what she preached, and some of the ladies felt that this would damage their cause.

What was this woman's dissent worth in the struggle for the emancipation of women? One writer, in a magazine article of that time, estimated that she had set back the suffrage cause at least 20 years, particularly in the Eastern United States. And in the same article, one lady was quoted as saying that the country people around her would not believe "that women want suffrage for anything but free love." To Victoria Woodhull, the physical bondage of woman was a form of slavery; to a Victorian society accustomed to the double standard, it was the natural order of things.

LINCOLN AND THE MEXICAN WAR

Abraham Lincoln, the young Congressman from Illinois, had condemned the war with Mexico as "unnecessarily and unconstitutionally commenced by the President." He introduced the so-called "spot resolution" in Congress, asking whether the spot where the Mexicans had attacked and spilled the blood of American troops was really United States territory. For his dissent, Lincoln drew the anger of a good many constituents for his "unpatriotic" stand, and Stephen A. Douglas, his future foe in a series of debates, had this to say: "You, sir, are a traitor, for referring to this war as unjust, immoral, and unconstitutional at a time when our boys are bleeding on foreign soil." In spite of his criticism of the war, Lincoln and others of the same viewpoint voted for funds to carry on the war, thinking, perhaps, that growing opposition to the war might turn the people against the Democrats.

THOREAU AND THE MEXICAN WAR

"How do you expect children to learn if you don't whip them?" The question was directed at the teacher, Henry David Thoreau, by members of the school committee. The question angered Thoreau, and to show the absurdity of the order that he must whip the students, the next day he picked out half a dozen and whipped them for no reason at all. That was the end of the teaching career of a man who lived according to his principles. Today, it is not Thoreau the teacher, but Thoreau the dissenter whose example is remembered by so many people.

To Thoreau, the war against Mexico was designed to please the slaveholding interests by adding parts of Mexico as slave territory. Because of this conviction, Thoreau refused to pay his poll tax and was sent to jail. How he felt about this experience is perhaps best expressed in his remark to his friend Ralph Waldo Emerson, who visited him in jail:

"Henry, what are you doing in there?" asked Emerson.
"Waldo, what are you doing out there?" replied Thoreau.

As it happened, Thoreau spent only one night in jail, but the incident and the ensuing essay "On the Duty of Civil Disobedience" have exerted a profound influence on the lives of many men. Thoreau is often quoted to justify causes today: "If the law is of such a nature that it requires you to be an agent of injustice to another, then I say, break the law. Let your life be a counter friction to stop the machine."

The Russian novelist Tolstoy was greatly influenced by Thoreau, as was Gandhi, the Hindu leader who developed the techniques of civil disobedience and nonviolence that eventually brought independence to India. In the United States, the whole civil-rights movement can be seen as an outgrowth of the ideas of Thoreau. The late leader of that movement, Martin Luther King, wrote:

During my early college days I read Thoreau's essay on civil disobedience for the first time. Fascinated by the idea of refusing to cooperate with an evil system, I was so deeply moved that I reread the work several times. I became convinced then that noncooperation with evil is as much a moral obligation as is cooperation with good.

THE TWENTIETH CENTURY

The Union victory in the Civil War brought freedom to the slaves, but it did not bring economic, political, or social equality to the Negro. There were some among the black community who felt that the Negro had to "earn" these freedoms by a gradual process of self-improvement. One such person was Booker T. Washington, the son of a mulatto slave, who became well-known for his association with Tuskegee Institute, a vocational college for Negroes. In his book *Up From Slavery* (1901), and in a widely publicized speech in Atlanta, the "Atlanta Compromise," Washington urged the Negro to seek economic equality before attempting to gain social equality. He wrote that "all the privileges that will come to us must be the result of severe and constant struggle rather than of artificial forcing." Forget about political power and civil rights, he urged, and go after industrial education and jobs. As for higher education, that could also come at a later time.

Washington's stand pleased many whites, but a strong dissent came from the pen of W. E. B. Du Bois, also of Negro parentage, a historian and sociologist, and founder of the National Association for the Advancement of Colored People (NAACP). Du Bois rejected completely the idea of gradualism, which he termed "submission." In reply to Washington's views, he wrote:

They [the Negro people] are absolutely certain that the way for a people to gain their reasonable rights is not by voluntarily throwing them away and insisting that they do not want them; that the way for a people to gain respect is not by continually belittling and ridiculing themselves; that on the contrary, Negroes must insist continually, in season and out of season, that voting is necessary to modern manhood, that color discrimination is barbarism, and that black boys need education as well as white boys.

As far as "earning" a place in society, Du Bois held that this would not come about in an atmosphere of prejudice and discrimination. He became so disgusted with the lack of progress in race relations that he joined the Communist party in 1961, and in 1963 left the United States for Ghana, where he died.

Today, the struggle for full equality still goes on, and the debate over ways and means to achieve that equality divides the Negro community now as in the past. But to some Negro leaders, the division is of little or no significance, for they feel that there are many paths to freedom.

WORLD WAR I

The First World War, the war to "make the world safe for democracy," was the target of widespread dissent. One who gained much attention for opposition to the war was Jeanette Rankin, the first woman to be elected to the House of Representatives. Miss Rankin had been active in the women's suffrage movement, but her "no" vote for declaring war on Germany on April 6, 1917 aroused the antifeminists to a high pitch. Another critic of the war was Eugene V. Debs, a socialist, who ran for President of the United States in 1900 and four times thereafter. His popular appeal was never very great, although in 1920 he received 919,000 votes. Debs was a pacifist, and when he spoke out against American intervention in World War I, he was sentenced to ten years in prison for violation of the Espionage Act. Debs' answer to his imprisonment may be found in these lines from "My Prison Breed":

While there is a lower class I am in it;
While there is a criminal element I am of it;
While there's a soul in prison I am not free.

Debs was not alone. Of the approximately 4,000 conscientious objectors in World War I, 500 were courtmartialed and convicted, 17 were sentenced to death (but all escaped the penalty), and 142 were sentenced to life imprisonment. Shortly after taking office in 1933, Franklin Roosevelt pardoned all those who were still in prison.

Prior to the United States intervention, there had been strong feeling against "meddling in European affairs." But as soon as American troops were involved, popular feeling for the war rose to great intensity, and a wave of patriotic songs and slogans swept across the nation, with such an effect that an "objector" became almost the same as a "traitor." German-American citizens were shunned by their neighbors. Orchestras stopped playing German music and schools dropped classes in the German language. The height of what one historian call the "national hysteria" was the comment of Theodore Roosevelt about clergymen who used the pulpit to express dissent over the war: "The clergyman who does not put the flag above the church had better close his church and keep it closed."

After the war, the Espionage Act [1] continued in effect, and the federal and state governments reacted to what has been called the "Red Scare" by conducting a vigorous drive against political dissenters; namely, communists, socialists, and anarchists. One reason for the "scare" was the success of the Bolshevik revolution in Russia (and the ensuing tyranny) plus the resulting fear that "it could happen here." Added to this was the anxiety caused by a series of bomb plantings, some successful, some not. In one case, more than 30 bombs were discovered by a postal worker, all addressed to high officials in government and business. No one was killed in this case. But in another, 38 persons were killed, hundreds injured, and thousands of dollars of property damage was incurred as a result of a bomb explosion in New York City on September 16, 1920.

The Attorney General at the time, A. Mitchell Palmer, reacted to public opinion. He ordered his agents to conduct a series of raids on clubs, cafés, pool halls, and private homes across the nation. Thousands were rounded up in these raids. Citizens who were arrested were turned over to the states for prosecution under syndicalist and sedition laws. Aliens were imprisoned by federal authorities and reserved for deportation hearings.

Constitutional guarantees were generally ignored. Homes were invaded without search warrants. Deportation hearings were handled as executive functions by immigration officers of the Department of Labor, and the usual procedural safeguards were not often granted to the defendant.

---

[1] The Espionage Act, passed in 1917, provided penalties for transmitting defense information to a foreign government and for other treasonable or disloyal activities.

People were deported on the slightest evidence of violation of the immigration code. Others were jailed, not for any overt act, but for opinions that were considered dangerous or objectionable for their own sake. In time the scare subsided, possibly because leaders of both political parties agreed with President Wilson that Americans could not solve the Nation's problems by stamping out unpopular political views.

After the outbreak of World War II, there was a strong sentiment in the United States for a "Yankee stay home" policy, particularly among members of the Communist party and among isolationist groups. But when the Germans violated the nonaggression pact with Russia, and invaded that country in June of 1941, the Communists changed their position. Most of the isolationists made the same switch after the Japanese attack on Pearl Harbor on December 7, 1941. From that point on, the United States fought a war with practically no organized protest at home. One example of the unanimity of feeling was that Jeanette Rankin (mentioned earlier in connection with her opposition to World War I) cast the only vote in the House of Representatives in opposition to the declaration of war against Germany and Japan.

One of the greatest assaults on freedom of expression and belief came in the years following World War II, when the House Un-American Activities Committee intensified its attack on subversion. The committee had been formed prior to the war as kind of a watchdog to determine if the foreign ideologies of Communism, Nazism, or Facism were taking hold in the United States. But it was not until the 1950's, under the leadership of Senator Joseph McCarthy of Wisconsin, that the Committee embarked on what same critics called the "greatest witch-hunt in our history."

The Senator claimed that the State Department was "thoroughly riddled with Communists." (Not one was ever found.) High officials in the Eisenhower administration were accused of being "soft on Communism" or "dupes of the Communists," or just plain pro-Communist. Individuals were singled out for attack. J. Robert Oppenheimer, one of the scientists responsible for the development of the atomic bomb, was excluded from his work on the Atomic Energy Commission because of an earlier association with Communists and because he opposed the development of the hydrogen bomb on "moral grounds." In another "guilt by association" case, the late Dr. Martin Luther King, Jr., was branded as a "Communist sympathizer" with information obtained from HUAC files. Dr. King had been photographed at the Highlander Folk School in Monteagle, Tennessee, a school of interracial education for 27 years. The school had been labeled a "Communist training school" in testimony before the HUAC by Southern segregationists. Pictures of King at the school were published as "proof" of the charges.

The Committee investigated all types of people for possible subversion: teachers, ministers, housewives, clerks. The widest publicity was given to persons called up to testify before the HUAC, and the very process of being given a subpoena often meant the loss of a job or a ruined reputation. There were even cases of uninvolved relatives who were fired from their jobs because of the relationship. If a witness was considered "unfriendly" by the Committee, he faced the possibility of a jail sentence, and almost certain economic or social sanctions.

Finally, when Senator McCarthy took on the army for "softness on Communism," the nation reacted against the reckless charges and accusations of this self-appointed inquisitor. In December of 1954, the Senate of the United States censured McCarthy for "acting contrary to senatorial ethics" and "obstructing the constitutional process of the Senate." From this point on, the Senator's influence declined, and most people came to realize the inconsistency of using police state methods to keep America the "land of the free."

This brief description of some former dissents is meant to provide an introduction to some of the dissents of today. What are the issues that now trouble the minds and hearts of "those who feel apart"? The readings in the following chapters should help clarify your own positions and may even change your mind, for, as the historian Herbert Muller wrote: "Once men begin examining the ideas they live by, there is no telling what they will come out with."

What Do You Think?

1. Is the right of dissent protected by the Constitution?
2. Why did Garrison burn a copy of the Constitution in public?
3. Some psychologists say that most people have a strong urge to conform. Do you think that is so?
4. It has been said that "the radical of yesterday is the conservative of today." What does this mean? Would you agree?
5. Does dissent become something else when it is accompanied by violence? Explain your reasoning.

Examples
of Dissent

What are some of the things that people do when they dissent? The following chapter will furnish a few examples.

Consider this question as you read: Is the dissent pictured a true reflection of our "national character" (if there is such a thing), or is it rather a reflection of the "fringe elements" in our society? Over a decade ago a British humorist, in attempting to satirize our "organizational" way of life, said that if three Americans were shipwrecked on an abandoned island, their first act would be to elect a president. If he had said that today, perhaps he might have added that if the election were successful, one of them would be picketing the other two. What do you think?

1.   "SUPPOSE THEY GAVE A WAR AND NO ONE CAME?" *

The following selection is written by the mother of a young man (Gene) who was arrested four times on charges related to pacifist activities. What factors led Gene to rebel?

In Gene's case, he grew up in a home part Quaker (Scott, my husband, born to another denomination, is now, by choice, a Quaker); part Jewish (me); all pacifist, but "respectably" pacifist. Scott and I had been antimilitarists in the 'thirties and had indeed worked hard upholding our beliefs, but never with the total commitment that is our son's way. When

---

* Excerpted from Charlotte E. Keyes, "Suppose They Gave a War and No One Came?" *McCall's Magazine,* October 1966. Copyright 1966 McCall Corporation. Reprinted by permission McIntosh and Otis, Inc.

World War II began, we regretfully felt that Hitlerism had to be fought with violence. It was not until 1945, four years after Gene was born, that we were drawn to learn more of the Quakers, because they knew no enemy and helped all with equal compassion.

How did Gene come to translate our peaceful ways into such uncompromising action? Was he always a rebel? people ask us. Yes, he was always a rebel, though a quiet and thoughtful one, from his schoolboy days. He was a fairly good student, interested in baseball, the high school paper, dramatics, and space travel. He always had friends—not a big circle, but warm and enduring ones.

Gene was always a worrier. He worried, from the time he was a very little boy, about the ants and flies and spiders I killed as I cleaned house. I laughed at him at first, until I remembered how Albert Schweitzer had lived with just such reverence for life, even to squeezing grapefruit juice on the floor for the ants to eat. I made the mistake of telling this to Gene, and sure enough, every morning, there was the ants' juice, squeezed for them on the kitchen floor.

In August, five months after arriving at New London, Gene was in jail. He and seven others had tried to swim to the submarine Ethan Allen. They had been stopped but not arrested and then had tried to reach the vessel by going through the main gate. This time, arrest had followed.

A telephone call from Gene the day before, and one from Marj Swann just after the arrest, kept us informed if not serene. Calls from local reporters who'd got the news from the wire services followed. This we'd been dreading, but found, to our relief, that the reporters were intelligent and objective, the stories written without slant or ridicule. One paper even quoted without comment such statements as this from a Polaris Action leaflet: " 'So the pacifist actionists cannot stay away from the Ethan Allen just because they been ordered to. Even if it means jail. They know that too many Germans were just obeying orders to look the other way. And they know that a Polaris submarine can cause more atrocities than 100 years of Auschwitz.' "

The papers also accurately printed Scott's and my comments: " 'Young people are more direct,' said Keyes, explaining the difference in the actions of parents and sons." "Worried but proud," they described me, and quoted, " 'I respect his decision, but I'm not sure civil disobedience is the best way to fight armament. I wish he were safe at home or safe in college.' "

Characteristically, Gene's first letter from jail began, "Having a fine time. Wish you were here."

We were happy to be able to write him that friends and even acquaintances had been going out of their way to express their love and sympathy. One friend who wanted to visit Gene at the jail on a trip East touched us very much, and when we thanked her with all our hearts; she said,

"I feel as though he's fighting our battles." Another friend phoned and bawled me out for not backing Gene up all the way. I was quite delighted to be scolded.

We had every kind of reaction to his stand. Telephone calls, of course, accusing him of being a Communist. One caller became quite interested when we pointed out that it would be impossible for a pacifist to be a Communist, because he can never engage in violent revolution and because he always puts the individual's relation to God and conscience above his relation to the state, as the early Christians did. The man ended by requesting that we let him see some of our peace literature. Not all conversations ended on this friendly note, however. One man said flatly that anybody who did not obey his country's laws was a traitor.

Strangers wrote letters pro and con to the local newspapers. One man put it: "He is an admitted criminal who openly defies our laws when they interfere with his personal beliefs."

But when another answered, saying that though he did not share Gene's beliefs, he defended his right to fight for them, he received a call from the antagonistic letter writer apologizing for his own letter.

The clock kept ticking inexorably, and in December, Gene came home primed for action. He had now a clear and concrete plan of a way to challenge the draft law so that people would become aware it could be challenged. It was his belief that this law was now accepted as being as much a part of our government as the Bill of Rights. He felt most of us did not realize that whether the draft continued or was abolished lay in the hands not of some mysterious and far-off government, but in the hands of us, the people. Only we needed a shock to make us realize it, since years of legal protest by peace workers and others had awakened very few. It was as Mildred Olmstead, of the Women's International League for Peace and Freedom, has said: "I have often wondered why it is that a family which would make a great protest if the government took away their automobile or even their dog, says nothing when the government takes away their sons."

In keeping with the pacifists' way of explaining all actions beforehand, Gene wrote a letter to the two local papers and told them what he planned to do: "Christmas Eve reminds us of our duty to work for peace on earth, a world without war. . . . As a prayer for peace on earth, I will be holding a vigil on Christmas Eve in front of the office of the local draft board. If I can withstand the weather, I hope to witness for twelve hours, beginning at noon. In any event, at midnight Christmas Eve, I will be using my I-A draft card to light a candle."

To burn his draft card! The idea was as new and shocking to us when he first described it as it still is to most people. At that time, though Gene was not the first to do this, there had not been many, and the whole action seemed preposterous to us.

He had talked with us and written us about this for a long time, and he listened as patiently as always to our protests. But the words of two others rang louder in his heart. There was the motto of William Lloyd Garrison's magazine, *The Liberator:* "Our country is the world—our countrymen are all mankind." And undergirding everything was Jesus' admonition: "Love your enemies, bless them that curse you, do good to them that hate you."

All I could turn to for help was the weather. I began to pray almost as hard for bad weather as Gene was praying for peace. I wanted a blizzard and temperature twenty below zero, weather even our quixotic son would admit was more than a human being could stand. But on December 24 the temperature rose. It was still cold, but had become short of unbearable. And at noon, he walked to the draft board and began his vigil.

He was dressed warmly and neatly, had on earmuffs and a dark-blue overcoat, and wore suspended from his shoulders a sign that read: "To Light This Candle with a Draft Card—A Prayer for Peace on Earth." The sign had been beautifully lettered by an artist friend. He was accompanied by his girl, who, for a large part of the day, kept vigil with him.

I was resigned and even, once again, as always seemed to happen when my worst fears were realized, proud.

All of us went there from time to time during the day to keep him company—our two younger sons and daughter and one son's girl, as well as Scott and I. Other friends unexpectedly came to accompany Gene for parts of the day. Even some strangers walked up and down with him now and again, not necessarily agreeing, but interested and eager to discuss. But, of course, Gene was the only one who kept vigil, and fasted, twelve long, cold hours.

At home, we were trying to go ahead with Christmas preparations—decorating the tree, wrapping presents. But we were tense and absent-minded and, as it grew late, were all at the draft board again. This time, a crowd of about twenty-five was there to watch. If any were unfriendly, they did not speak up. TV cameramen and reporters were also waiting.

At midnight, there was a stir; the cameramen and others got ready to snap the scene. Gene's girl began to play her part—holding the candle while he got the draft card ready in a pair of tongs. He took out a cigarette lighter, but a bitter wind kept blowing out the flame.

I began praying again—Don't let this look ridiculous. It's so important to him! Oh, let it light! And at last the card and the candle were lit. The card burned quickly in the grip of the tongs.

I let go my breath. It was over. People crowded around. Some were nervously laughing, and some were almost crying. I was doing a little of both.

Scott went to Gene and patted his back, much as he used to do when our son was little and succeeded in something he'd been afraid to do, like climbing a high tree. I held him in my arms a moment. We had no words. But he knew both of us were close to him.

And so it has become. As we have watched him grow and climb his high places, we no longer argue with him, no longer call him foolish. We stand by our son, and we learn from him.

What Do You Think?

1. Was Congress right in making it a crime to burn a draft card? Why or why not?
2. What inspires people like Gene to act in this way?

2. "I WILL NO LONGER CARRY A DRAFT CARD." *

There are many conscientious objectors who oppose the draft in peacetime as well as wartime. What does this letter to a local draft board suggest about the causes of dissent?

Local Board No. 114
Middlesex County
34 Commonwealth Ave.
West Concord, Mass.

Gentlemen:

I am writing to return my draft card and to inform you that I am no longer able to comply with the Selective Service System. I will no longer carry a draft card or comply with any directives from the Selective Service System. To do so would be to violate the dictates of my conscience and thus do a disservice to myself, my country, and humanity . . .

I understand that by refusing to comply with the Selective Service System I will be breaking the law. I understand that the penalties imposed by the government on "non-cooperators" have not been light and for a long time this knowledge has prevented me from severing my connection with Selective Service. For a long time I thought that I could rest with an easy conscience if only I could establish recognition as a conscientious objector. I felt that it was participation in the military that I was rejecting and not conscription itself. I thought that as long as I was not compelled

---

* Reprinted from *The Draft?*, a report prepared by the American Friends Service Committee, published by Hill and Wang Company, New York, 1968.

to participate directly in a system that has been established to do violence to human beings (like most violence, done in the name of freedom, justice, and self-defense), that as long as I could be assured of exemption from this system, I need not resist registration with the Selective Service System.

The political or practical basis for my disobedience relates, again, to my conception of work "in the national interest." As I see it, the work that I am doing as a draft counselor with the American Friends Service Committee is not only in the national interest, it is in the interest of all of humanity. Resisting evil, in whatever form it takes, is in the best interest of mankind. By resisting the draft I am combatting the first ranks in the forces of an evil system—the military—that affects all young men throughout the United States.

I will try to make clear some of the more practical reasons why I feel that the military and conscription must be resisted. The evil effects of conscription are so numerous as to be impossible to catalog in detail, but some of its most destructive aspects are these:

1. The draft forces young men to become part of the military machine, the primary purpose of which is to kill human beings. The draft forces young men—at a critical time in their lives, during which they are exploring values and trying to establish their own ethical orientations—to acquiesce to and participate in the military establishment which has its own uniquely pernicious value system that reverses most of the positive and creative values of humanity and undermines their influence in the lives of America's youth.

The best soldier, the Armed Forces teach us—contrary to our Christian tradition of values—is the most efficient murderer. The feeble voice of humanity's "Thou shalt not kill," is drowned out by the sergeant's roaring "Thou shalt kill and kill well!"

"All men are brothers," we learn in our Sunday Schools. But the Army teaches, "The best soldier is the one who makes the clearest distinction between the 'good guys.' The best soldier realizes soonest that all men are brothers except the 'Japs,' the 'Krauts,' the 'Commies,' the 'VC.' "

The best soldier ignores religion, God, and his conscience and learns to "follow orders." The best soldier can kill without thinking twice about it because he realizes that it is "his job" to do so.

These are values that our society has decided to instill into the minds, hearts, and reflexes of its youth. These are the values that I must reject. These are the values that are contrary to "the national interest." This is why draft resistance is work in "the national interest," and in the interest of all humanity.

2. The deferment system is an elitist system that serves the wealthy and privileged and feeds on the less prestigious. The draft

obligation subtly forces the nation's youth into positions that a few power holders and policy makers deem to be in the "national interest," obliging them to move into professional and academic careers that they may not have chosen except for the fact that the military is their only alternative if they drop out of school. These inequities and manipulative "channeling" techniques are widely acknowledged and I need not expand on them here. . . .

What Do You Think?

1. How can a government tell whether "conscientious objectors" are sincere or not?
2. If you were a member of Local Board 114, how would you react to this young man's letter? Explain.
3. Should conscientious objectors be excused from military service? Why or why not?
4. How might Gene (see Reading 1) react to this letter?

3.   "THE GOVERNMENT IS . . . TAKING AWAY OUR RELIGIOUS FREEDOM." *

One of the strongest arguments for compulsory school attendance is that a democracy depends on an enlightened electorate in order to function. There is some question, however, as to how long this "enlightenment" takes. The Amish people think that eight years is sufficient, particularly because they fear that their children's religious beliefs will be "corrupted" by the high school curriculum and social life. Also, the Amish live entirely apart in their own communities, and do not care whether their children learn science, or civics, or history. Here is how one Amish community "dissented" when faced with compulsory public school attendance for their children.

LeRoy Garber, a short, muscular Amishman of 41, can be laconic, as the Amish often are with outsiders. But on the subject of schooling for his children, he has a lot to say. He says it with so much conviction that the beard jutting out from his chin jabs the air like a conductor's baton.

"The Supreme Court's decision, or I should say the Court's undecision,

---

* Excerpted from John Morton, "All Amish Lost a Little Ground in the Decision," *The National Observer,* October 30, 1967.

is not going to change my way of thinking or my belief," he told me in the sparsely furnished living-room of his farm home six miles southwest of Hutchinson.

He was referring to the U. S. Supreme Court's refusal last week to accept jurisdiction over an appeal of his conviction on a charge of failing to keep his daughter Sharon in school. He had been arrested when Sharon was 15 under a new Kansas law that requires school attendance to age 16, rather than through the eighth grade as under the old law.

A LEGAL PRECEDENT

The decision may have wide implications for the 50,000 Amish in the United States, who believe generally that school past the eighth grade in "too worldly" for their children. Many states that have held up rigid enforcement of attendance laws may now feel they have a legal precedent to seize upon.

For Mr. Garber the court's refusal means that he must pay the $5 fine and $64.25 in court costs imposed on him in the District Court of Reno County, Kansas, after his conviction in January, 1966.

Looming large in his protest against high school are the social activities and the free-wheeling youth who would be rubbing shoulders with his children every day. The Amish are greatly afraid that their children will learn "worldly ways" that would lead them away from their religion, and school is the one place where the Amish parents cannot control the relationships of their children.

While Mr. Garber has been the most militant of the Kansas Amish so far, there are others who are slowly, seriously deciding whether to compromise the "old ways" on the school question or face criminal action. . . .

Mr. Showalter, a Missouri Synod Lutheran with Mennonite forebears, who has lived among Amish for 35 years, says: "You're going to have both kinds of reaction to this. Some of them are going to send their children to school and some of them are going to pay fines or sit in jail." . . .

The "Amish problem," which one educator has said "like death and taxes, will always be with us," has troubled several states. The Amish are most heavily concentrated in Pennsylvania, where they first settled in this country, and in Ohio and Indiana. They are found in lesser numbers in Kansas, Michigan, Iowa, Kentucky, and Delaware. They live in 19 states in all.

In Iowa two years ago, Amish were jailed and their children chased into a cornfield when state officials demanded compliance with attendance laws. The confrontations have not been so dramatic elsewhere, but they have occurred.

COMMUNITY LEAVES

Last December, an entire Amish community (most communities contain about 25 families) in Bruno, Ark., sold out and moved to British Honduras. They had moved to Arkansas originally in 1949 because they felt other states had become too sophisticated. Arkansas, which had attendance laws it was not enforcing, did not bother the community in Bruno, and the Amish leaders expressed their appreciation of this as they left. But their leaders said the experiences in Iowa and the trend of the country generally pointed to more and more difficulties for the Amish way of life. Harold Stoll, bishop of the Bruno group, complained: "The government is gradually taking away our religious freedom."

What Do You Think?

1.   Why does Mr. Garber call the court ruling an "undecision"?
2.   Should there be any limits to religious freedom? Why or why not? If you think so, what should these limits entail?
3.   When religious freedom comes into conflict with laws set down by the state, which should prevail? Why?
4.   In most instances, school districts receive money from the state in relation to student enrollment. In other words, the more students, the more money to run the school district. Do you think this is relevant to the Amish situation?

4.   "THIS BILL WILL LIVE IN INFAMY." *

George C. Wallace, who ran for President in the 1968 campaign, has been one of the loudest voices of dissent over recent decisions of the Supreme Court, and, more specifically, the Civil Rights Act of 1964. What causes Mr. Wallace to dissent?

We come here today in deference to the memory of those stalwart patriots who on July 4, 1776, pledged their lives, their fortunes, and their sacred honor to establish and defend the proposition that governments are created by the people, empowered by the people, derive their just powers from the consent of the people, and must forever remain subservient to the will of the people.

Today, 188 years later, we celebrate that occasion and find inspira-

---

* George C. Wallace, "The Civil Rights Bill: Fraud, Sham, and Hoax," speech in Atlanta, Georgia, 1964, reprinted in *Voices of Crisis,* edited by Floyd Matson, Odyssey Press, N. Y., 1967.

tion and determination and courage to preserve and protect the great principles of freedom enunciated in the Declaration of Independence.

It is therefore a cruel irony that the President of the United States has only yesterday signed into law the most monstrous piece of legislation ever enacted by the United States Congress.

It is a fraud, a sham, and a hoax.

This bill will live in infamy. To sign it into law at any time is tragic. To do so upon the eve of the celebration of our independence insults the intelligence of the American people.

It dishonors the memory of countless thousands of our dead who offered up their very lives in defense of principles which this bill destroys.

Never before in the history of this nation have so many human and property rights been destroyed by a single enactment of the Congress. It is an act of tyranny. It is the assassin's knife struck in the back of liberty.

With this assassin's knife and a blackjack in the hand of the federal force-cult, the left-wing liberals will try to force us back into bondage. Bondage to a tyranny more brutal than that imposed by the British Monarchy which claimed power to rule over the lives of our forefathers under sanction of the divine right of kings.

Today, this tyranny is imposed by the central government which claims the right to rule over our lives under sanction of the omnipotent black-robed despots who sit on the bench of the United States Supreme Court.

This bill is fraudulent in intent, in design, and in execution.

It is misnamed. Each and every provision is mistitled. It was rammed through the Congress on the wave of ballyhoo, promotions, and publicity stunts reminiscent of P. T. Barnum.

It was enacted in an atmosphere of pressure, intimidation, and even cowardice, as demonstrated by the refusal of the United States Senate to adopt an amendment to submit the bill to a vote of the people.

To illustrate the fraud—it is not a civil rights bill. It is a federal penal code. It creates federal crimes which would take volumes to list and years to tabulate because it affects the lives of 192 million American citizens. Every person in every walk and station of life and every aspect of our daily lives becomes subject to the criminal provisions of this bill.

It threatens our freedom of speech, of assembly, or association, and makes the exercise of these freedoms a federal crime under certain conditions.

It affects our political rights, our right to trial by jury, our right to the full use and enjoyment of our private property, the freedom from search and seizure of our private property and possessions, the freedom from harassment by federal police and, in short, all the rights of individuals inherent in a society of free men.

Now on the subject of the court let me make it clear that I am not attacking any member of the United States Supreme Court as an individual. However, I do attack their decisions; I question their intelligence, their common sense and their judgment; I consider the federal judiciary system to be the greatest single threat to individual freedom and liberty in the United States today, and I'm going to take off the gloves in talking about these people.

There is only one word to describe the federal judiciary today. That word is "lousy."

They assert more power than claimed by King George III, more power than Hitler, Mussolini, or Khrushchev ever had. They assert the power to declare unconstitutional our very thoughts. To create for us a system of moral and ethical values. To outlaw and declare unconstitutional, illegal, and immoral the customs, traditions, and beliefs of the people, and furthermore they assert the authority to enforce their decrees in all these subjects upon the American people without their consent.

What Do You Think?

1.   Is it possible to legislate in matters of social justice? Desirable?
2.   Education is usually thought to be a function of the state, not of the federal government. Did the Supreme Court have the right to order desegregation of the schools in 1954? What determines "right" in such cases?
3.   Would you consider George Wallace a dissenter?

5.   WHAT DO THESE WOMEN WANT? *

It has been estimated that women make up approximately 51 per cent of our population, yet many women feel that they more rightly belong in the status of a minority group because they are discriminated against on the basis of sex. If this is true, what should be done about the problem? Is it the proper function of government to tell an employer that he must pay a woman the same salary as a man, or should women fight their own battles on the labor front?

It was billed as a black comedy, nothing elaborate. Twelve comely feminists, dressed for cocktails, would crash the hearings of the Equal Employment Opportunities Commission on sex discrimination in employ-

---

* Excerpted from Martha Weinman Lear, "The Second Feminist Wave," *The New York Times Magazine,* March 10, 1968. Reprinted with the permission of Martha Weinman Lear and *The New York Times Magazine.*

ment. They would make some noise, possibly get arrested, certainly get thrown out, meet the press, and all the while give prominent display to large, home-lettered signs, of which my favorite read: "A Chicken in Every Pot, a Whore in Every Home."

The feminists were members of the New York chapter of NOW (a multilayered acronym: The National Organization for Women, which wants "full equality for all women in America, in truly equal partnership with men," now). To the press, they would explain that they were pro-testing all those prejudices and laws of the land which keep women at home and in the bottom of the job market, but exclude them from jobs that utilize intelligence in any significant way.

This makes it clear, they would say, that women are valued not for their intelligence but only for their sexuality—i.e., as wives and mothers —which, stripping the matter of its traditional sacred cows, reduces the Women's Role to a sort of socially acceptable whoredom. . . .

By compromise, 12 "whores" metamorphosed into two secretaries who picketed the E. E. O. C. several weeks back, literally chained to their typewriters. This made a precise point in an eminently respectable way, and the press coverage was good.

Shortly before that, NOW members had picketed *The New York Times* in protest against the "Help Wanted—Male" and "Help Wanted—Female" column headings in classified advertising. They maintained these designations violate Title VII of the Civil Rights Act of 1964, which prohibits sex discrimination in employment. The E. E. O. C. permits such column headings, by a logic which seems capricious to feminists and complex to almost everyone. NOW representatives met with officials of *The Times*. ("We told them," one feminist said, "that those column headings perpetuate the employment ghetto." "We told them," said Monroe Green, then *The Times* vice-president in charge of advertising, "that if we discontinued the column headings there might be fewer jobs for women because men would be applying for them. After all, men can be just as militant as women.") Nothing swayed, the NOW people recently an-nounced that they are bringing suit against the E. E. O. C. to get a ruling on the matter.

They also are helping two stewardesses' unions fight for the right of an airline hostess to stay on the job after she dodders past her 32nd birthday. In New York, they are pushing for the repeal of all state abortion laws. In Washington, they are lobbying for passage of a civil-rights amendment for women, which has been getting tossed out of every Congress since 1923. In various states they have pending court cases which will test the validity of so-called "protective laws" (i.e., women may work only so many hours; women may lift only so many pounds). NOW says these laws are obsolescent and keep women from earning more money and getting better jobs.

What NOW wants, by way of immediate implementation of its goals, is total enforcement of Title VII; a nationwide network of child-care centers, operating as optional community facilities; revision of the tax laws to permit full deduction of housekeeping and child-care expenses for working parents; maternity benefits which would allow some period of paid maternity leave and guarantee a woman's right to return to her job after childbirth; revision of divorce and alimony laws ("so that unsuccessful marriages may be terminated without hypocrisy, and new ones contracted without undue financial hardship to either man or woman"), and a Constitutional Amendment withholding Federal funds from any agency, institution, or organization discriminating against women. . . .

"The institution of marriage has the same effect the institution of slavery had. It separates people in the same category, disperses them, keeps them from identifying as a class. The masses of slaves didn't recognize their condition, either. To say that a woman is really 'happy' with her home and kids is as irrelevant as saying that the blacks were 'happy' being taken care of by Ol' Massa. She is defined by her maintenance role. Her husband is defined by his productive role. We're saying that all human beings should have a productive role in society." . . .

Says Betty Friedan . . . "It may be that we are asking too much of it [marriage], and that almost inevitably it will become a straitjacket for both sexes. The inefficacy of all this tinkering, the assumption of 'Can this marriage be saved?' makes you want to vomit.

"We work with the realities of American life, and in reality our job now is to make it possible for women to integrate their roles at home and in society. But as to whether we will finally have to challenge the institutions, the concepts of marriage and the nuclear family—I don't know. I just don't know.

"What I do know is this: If you agree that women are human beings who should be realizing their potential, then no girl child born today should responsibly be brought up to be a housewife. Too much has been made of defining human personality and destiny in terms of the sex organs. After all, we share the human brain."

What Do You Think?

1. Should men be paid higher salaries than women? Explain.
2. During the Great Depression, many people suggested that "working wives" should be fired. Do you agree?
3. Why is there such a small percentage of women in Congress?
4. Does marriage "enslave" women?
5. There is an organization of women dedicated to gaining the acceptance of a woman's right to have children without mar-

riage, and, above all, the right to call these children "legitimate." Do you go along with this?

ACTIVITIES FOR INVOLVEMENT

1. Role play an imaginary situation in which two students portray individuals discussing Gene's decision to burn his draft card. (see Reading 1) One student might portray an individual who tries to talk Gene out of the act, while the second lends his support.

2. Research and report orally to the class on other draft-card burnings which have occurred throughout the United States in the last few years. In what ways are the reasons given for these actions similar to Gene's? Different?

3. Below are listed a number of ways by which individuals might dissent from policies or actions with which they do not approve. Rank these in order of what you think is their *effectiveness,* placing those which you believe to be most capable of *bringing about change* at the top, and those which you believe to be least effective at the bottom. Then explain why you ranked the items as you did.

· Speaking out against policies or action with which one disagrees.
· "Sitting-in" at lunch counters to protest discriminatory hiring practices.
· *Threatening* others with physical harm.
· Using violence when necessary.
· Voting against government officials.
· Refusing to vote.
· "Dropping out."
· Doing one's own "thing."
· Leaving the country.

4. Write a short paper or hold a debate on the topic: "When, if ever, should dissent be forbidden?" Be sure to explain the reasoning behind the views you express.

5. Review each of the examples of dissent presented in this chapter. Imagine that you were asked to argue *against* each of these dissenters. What would you say? How do you suppose each of the dissenters would reply?

6. Make a list of all the forces which exist in American society today which you believe contribute to dissent today. Compare your list with others prepared by your classmates and then draw up a master list. After reading Chapter 4, add any that you may have omitted. Then hold a class discussion on which of these forces are beneficial or destructive today, and why.

Causes
of Dissent

This chapter will indicate some of the causes for the dissent that is taking place in the United States today. Young people figure prominently in this dissent, but there are also other groups and individuals protesting what they feel to be economic or social injustice, or the policies of the government. What other causes can you add?

1. RACIAL INJUSTICE *

Of the many minorities who came to America, most of them were at first the targets of prejudice and bigotry, but eventually all were assimilated into the mainstream of American life. The Negro, who came against his will, is still an outsider. In the following selection, the late Dr. Martin Luther King expresses a deep-felt concern that time is running out.

Through scientific and technological advances we have made of this world and our nation a neighborhood. Through our ethical commitments we have failed to make of it a brotherhood. So we find ourselves suffering from a kind of poverty of the spirit which stands in glaring contrast to our scientific and technological abundance. We've learned to fly the air like birds, swim the seas like fish and yet we haven't learned the simple art of walking the earth as brothers and sisters. This is a great tragedy and a great challenge of the hour, for let me assure you that if

---

* Excerpted from Dr. Martin Luther King, "Martin Luther King at the Fairmont," an address by Dr. King published in FOCUS, by station KQED, San Francisco.

we don't learn to live together in this nation as brothers we are all going to perish together as fools.

Racial injustice still is the black man's burden and the white man's shame. On the Statute of Liberty we read that America is the mother of the exile—the white exile from Europe. It has never had the same maternal concern and care for the black exiles who were brought to this country in chains from Africa. This is why our forebears could sing "Sometimes I Feel like a Motherless Child." A great sense of estrangement and rejection caused the Negro to use such a metaphor.

FREEDOM TO HUNGER

In 1863 the Negro was granted freedom from the shackles of slavery through the Emancipation Proclamation. He wasn't given any land to make that freedom mean anything. That was almost like having a man in jail for 30 to 40 years and pretty soon you discover that he's innocent of the charge he's been convicted of. You come up to him one day saying you are not guilty and now you are free. At the same time you refuse to give him any bus fare to get to town, refuse to give him any money to buy clothes, to get shoes for his feet. Any system of jurisprudence rises up against it. Yet this is what happened to the black man. He was told he was free, but he was penniless; he was illiterate, standing around not knowing where to go and what to do. We must never forget that at that same moment America was giving millions of acres of land away in the West and Midwest. America was willing to undergird its white peasants with an economic floor. It refused to undergird its black peasants from Africa with an economic floor. So freedom for the Negro was freedom without bread to eat and land to cultivate. It was freedom and famine at the same time. The fact is that America has been backlashing on the question of genuine equality for the black man for more than 300 years.

THE INVISIBLE POOR

Fifty per cent of Negro families live in our country in substandard housing conditions. They live in slums, hemmed in, in the ghetto. And in that ghetto we pay more for less. Our sons and daughters graduate from high school, thousands reading at the sixth or eighth grade level, not because they don't have native intelligence, but because the schools are so inadequate, so disorderly, so segregated. So we find this culture of poverty. The problem is so often that we don't see the poor—some Negroes of the middle class who somehow sailed out of the muddy waters and moved into the fresh flowing waters of the mainstream. They've forgotten the sense of the backwaters. In the ghettos our black brothers and sisters are as bitter and feel as estranged from the Negro middle class as they do from white society.

WHO CAUSES RIOTS

Ultimately a great nation is a compassionate nation. There are snares in our society that cause misguided action and riots in many instances. Now you know my view about riots. They fail socially, are destructive and self-defeating. I will continue to raise my voice against riots because I think they do more harm to the Negro himself than anything or anybody else. Therefore my motto can't be "burn, baby, burn"— my motto must be build, baby, build. Organize, baby, organize. Black people of this country, it is high time now that America pays attention.

It is time to tell the nation who is really causing the riots. Riots are caused by nice, gentle, timid white moderns who are more concerned about order than justice, who can always say the Negro is pushing things too fast—wait for a more convenient season, who has a kind of paternalistic notion that he can set the timetables for the Negroes. Riots are caused by every labor union who will keep the Negro locked out, by many white clergymen who in the midst of social injustice prefer to remain silent behind the safe security of stained glass windows. Riots are caused by every state legislature that refuses to pass a fair housing bill.

There is nothing more dangerous than to build a society with a large segment of that society feeling that they have no status. A destructive minority can poison the wellspring from which the majority must drink. It is time for everybody to see this. America can solve this problem. We have the money—the richest nation in the world. The question isn't whether we have the resources, the question is whether we have the will. If our nation can spend 35 billion a year to fight a war in Vietnam and 20 billion a year to put a man on the moon, it can spend billions to put God's own children on their own two feet right here on earth.

I'm not going to despair even on the race question. Our goal is freedom and somehow I still believe that we're going to get there because the goal of America is freedom. Scorned though we may be, our destiny is tied up with the destiny of America. So let us keep going, however difficult it is. If you can't fly—run; if you can't run—walk; if you can't walk—crawl. But by all means, keep moving.

What Do You Think?

1. Are riots caused by "nice, timid white moderns" as Dr. King suggested? Explain.

2. Which is more important—order or justice? And what do these abstract words mean, anyway?

3. Dr. King has stated that the black man's destiny is tied up

with the destiny of America. Would you agree? Why or why not?

4.   What does this reading suggest may be at least one cause for dissent in this country?

2.   THE SQUARE WORLD *

The following selection is from a hippie newspaper printed in the Haight-Ashbury district of San Francisco. What does it suggest about the reasons for dissent today?

It is strange and disturbing to watch the straight community's angry, sometimes violent reaction to the hippies. There are many reasons for this. The principal one is appearance. The hippies dress strangely. They dress this way because they have thrown a lot of middle-class notions out the window and with them the most sensitive middle-class dogma: the neutral appearance.

The straight world is a jungle of taboos, fears, and personality games. People in that jungle prey on each other mercilessly. Therefore to survive in any jungle requires good protective coloring: the camouflage of respectable appearance. The anonymity of middle-class dress is like a flag of truce. It means (whether true or not): "I'm not one of the predators." It is in the nature of an assurance of harmlessness. Unusual or bright colored clothing, then, becomes an alarm, a danger signal to the fearful and their armed truce with the rest of mankind. They see it as a challenge. They are fearful, unsure of themselves, and fear sours into anger. It is but a step to thinking that the anger is "good." The oldest fallacy in the world is that anything that makes you angry must be bad.

The sin of the hippies is that they will not play the straight game of camouflage. Their non-participation, in effect, exposes them as "another tribe": whose disregard of straight taboos of dress makes them seem to be capable of anything, and therefore a danger. That danger moreover is felt clear up to city hall, that shrine of Squaredom. Why else, I submit, does the Health Department of this city have such a tender solicitude about the living conditions of human beings at the Haight when they have ignored the conditions at Hunter's Point, The Mission, and the Fillmore?

Many people cannot understand the hippies' rejection of everything that is commonly expected of the individual in regard to employment and life goals: steady lucrative employment, and the accumulation through the years of possessions and money, building (always building) security

---

* From an editorial in the *Haight Ashbury Maverick,* November 4, 1968.

for the future. It is precisely this security hypochrondria, this checking of bank books rather than pulses, this worrying over budgets instead of medicine cabinets, that drives the youth of today away. It is this frantic concern with money, that there will be enough of it, that the children start worrying about the always threatening future, that drives the young into the Haight Ashbury. They have seen their parents slave for years, wasting away a lifetime to make sure that the house was paid off, that the kids got through school in order to get "good" jobs so that they could join the frantic scramble, later on. The parents' reward for this struggle is that they wind up old and tired, alienated from their children and just as often each parent from the other. They have thought so long in terms of money and possessions, that they have forgotten how to think in terms of people. So they think of "my son," and "my daughter," and talk to their children as one would speak from a great distance to a checkbook.

"But you've got to build a future for yourself. If you don't support yourself, no one else is going to!" The tired, lined face argues to the young. "It's a hard world." And pray tell who makes it hard, participating in the scramble for material "security"? Who makes it difficult by insisting that everyone must participate in that scramble or suffer social censure? Listen to the tone of those who lecture about the "economic realities" of life. Are they presenting impartial facts? Or do they sound like someone expounding church doctrine? It is the latter. The conventional folk of our society, the "normal" people, so called, who believe in the rat race. Competition is holy. Keeping up with the Joneses is a mandate from God. The requirement of keeping up a respectable front is the principle article of faith.

It has been demonstrated over and over again throughout history by the best possible people that very little is required for happiness. It is the fight for money and possessions and the prestige they bring that sets people at odds, and that is what makes the world hard. We are the richest nation in the world, with the highest living standard. By our own fond illusions about prosperity we should also be the happiest. Are we? Suicides, racial violence, and the exodus of the young from comfortable homes suggest otherwise. The terrible truth is that our prosperity is the bringer of misery. We have been brainwashed by the advertising industry into being the most dissatisfied people in the world. We are told we must all be handsome or beautiful, sexually devastating, and owners of a staggering amount of recreational gadetry or doomed to frustration. The result is that most of us are frustrated. It is exactly this that the hippie avoids like poison. He wants no part of self-defeating goals.

It is very likely that the hippie will go hungry and suffer exposure, and perhaps freak out. But he considers these far less dangerous than the kind of dehumanization society tried to wreck on him before his rebellion.

He has escaped from a culture where the machine is god, and men judge each other by mechanical standards of efficiency and usefulness. He sees a madness in the constant fight to sell more washing machines, cars, toilet paper, girdles, and gadgets than the other fellow. He is equally horrified at the grim ruthlessness of the men who participate in that fight.

What Do You Think?

1. What are "taboos"? Why do the hippies object to them?
2. Is a cooperative society possible?
3. Why has the "straight" community reacted so violently to the hippies?

3. THE DOCTRINE OF WHITE SUPREMACY *

Earlier, you read a statement by the late Dr. Martin Luther King. The following selection, from the Autobiography of Malcolm X, *deals with the same topic, but there are significant differences. On one of these—Christianity—how do you think Dr. King (who was a Christian and a minister) would have answered Malcolm X?*

I tried in every speech I made to clarify my new position regarding white people—"I don't speak against the sincere, well-meaning, good white people. I have learned that there are some. I have learned that not all white people are racists. I am speaking against and my fight is against the white racists. I firmly believe that Negroes have the right to fight against these racists, by any means that are necessary."

But the white reporters kept wanting me linked with that word "violence." I doubt if I had one interview without having to deal with that accusation.

I am for violence if non-violence means we continue postponing a solution to American black man's problem—just to avoid violence. I don't go for non-violence if it also means a delayed solution. To me a delayed solution is a non-solution. Or I'll say it another way. If it must take violence to get the black man his human rights in this country, I'm for violence exactly as you know the Irish, the Poles, or Jews would be if they were flagrantly discriminated against. I am just as they would be in that case, and they would be for violence—no matter what the consequences, no matter who was hurt by the violence.

---

* Excerpted from Malcolm X, *Autobiography of Malcolm X,* New York, N. Y.: Grove Press. Reprinted by permission of Grove Press. Copyright © 1964 by Alex Haley and Malcolm X. Copyright © 1965 by Alex Haley and Betty Shabazz.

White society hates to hear anybody, especially a black man, talk about the crime the white man has perpetrated on the black man. I have always understood that's why I have been so frequently called "a revolutionist." It sounds as if I have done some crime! Well, it may be the American black man does need to become involved in a real revolution. The word for "revolution" in German is *Umwalzung*. What it means is a complete overturn—a complete change. The overthrow of King Farouk in Egypt and the succession of President Nasser is an example of a true revolution. It means the destroying of an old system, and its replacement with a new system. Another example is the Algerian revolution, led by Ben Bella; they threw out the French who had been there over 100 years. So how does anybody sound talking about the Negro in America waging some "revolution"? Yes, he is condemning a system—but he's not trying to overturn the system, or to destroy it. The Negro's so-called "revolt" is merely an asking to be accepted into the existing system! A true Negro revolt might entail, for instance, fighting for separate black states within this country—which several groups and individuals have advocated, long before Elijah Muhammad came along.

When the white man came into this country, he certainly wasn't demonstrating any "non-violence." In fact, the very man whose name symbolizes non-violence here today has stated:

"Our nation was born in genocide when it embraced the doctrine that the original American, the Indian, was an inferior race. Even before there were large numbers of Negroes on our shores, the scar of racial hatred had already disfigured colonial society. From the sixteenth century forward, blood flowed in battles over racial supremacy. We are perhaps the only nation which tried as a matter of national policy to wipe out its indigenous population. Moreover, we elevated that tragic experience into a noble crusade. Indeed, even today we have not permitted ourselves to reject or to feel remorse for this shameful episode. Our literature, our films, our drama, our folklore all exalt it. Our children are still taught to respect the violence which reduced a red-skinned people of an earlier culture into a few fragmented groups herded into impoverished reservations."

"Peaceful coexistence!" That's another one the white man has always been quick to cry. Fine! But what have been the deeds of the white man? During his entire advance through history, he has been waving the banner of Christianity . . . and carrying in his other hand the sword and the flintlock.

You can go right back to the very beginning of Christianity. Catholicism, the genesis of Christianity as we know it to be presently constituted, with its hierarchy, was conceived in Africa—by those whom the Christian church calls "The Desert Father." The Christian church became infected with racism when it entered white Europe. The Christian church returned to Africa under the banner of the Cross—conquering, killing, exploiting, pillaging, raping, bullying, beating—and teaching white supremacy. This is how the white man thrust himself into the position of leadership of the World—through the use of naked physical power. And he was totally inadequate spiritually. Mankind's history has proved from one era to another that the true criterion of leadership is spiritual. Men are attracted by spirit. By power, men are forced. Love is engendered by spirit. By power, anxieties are created.

I am in agreement one hundred per cent with those racists who say that no government laws ever can force brotherhood. The only true world solution today is governments guided by true religion—of the spirit. Here in race-torn America, I am convinced that the Islam religion is desperately needed, particularly by the American black man. The black man needs to reflect that he has been America's most fervent Christian— and where has it gotten him? In fact, in the white man's hands, in the white man's interpretation . . . where has Christianity brought this world?

It has brought the non-white two-thirds of the human population to rebellion. Two-thirds of the human population today is telling the one-third minority white man, "Get out!" And the white man is leaving. And as he leaves, we see the non-white peoples returning in a rush to their original religions, which had been labeled "pagan" by the conquering white man. Only one religion—Islam—had the power to stand and fight the white man's Christianity for a thousand years! Only Islam could keep the white Christianity at bay . . .

What Do You Think?

1. Would you agree with Malcolm X that the white man practiced genocide on the American Indian?
2. If peaceful means of dissent fail, is violence justified?
3. For a true revolution to take place, must *all* of the old system be destroyed? Why or why not?
4. What does this reading have to do with dissent?

4. THE WAR *

The following is a letter received by the Executive Director of the Episcopal Fellowship. The writer is an American volunteer worker for the United States AID (Agency for International Development)

---

* Reprinted from "You Aren't A Gook, Are You?" published by the American Friends Service Committee, 2160 Lake, San Francisco.

program in South Vietnam. How might someone in favor of the Vietnam war respond to this dissent?

Hue, Vietnam
1/23/67

Dear Friends,

This is going to be a rather emotional newsletter, I fear. The work here at the Animal Husbandry Station is going along satisfactorily and I have gone out into the countryside several times and visited some places in Hue. My work here is quite similar to any Peace Corpsman's who works in Agriculture; except for one thing. I find myself working in a country visited by war.

Do you know what that means? Can you even begin to imagine the utter horror and indescribable suffering that the word represents. WAR. The United States is fighting a war to prevent South Vietnam from being taken over by the Communists. I am here to tell you, my dear brethren, that if I were a poor Vietnamese peasant in this day, only *death* would prevent me from being a Vietnamese Communist. Do you understand that?

Do you understand what it means to have a plane fly overhead and just stop in utter terror of what that plane might be doing? Do you understand what napalm does to people? It explodes and spreads a jelly all over everything in the vicinity. This jelly is on fire. It burns through clothing and destroys the skin with burns. It leaves the people not already dead to die a horrible death by burns. It burns trees, houses, everything. Do you understand what a phosphorus bomb does? It gets on the body and burns; and it does not stop burning until it reaches bone. What does it feel like, I wonder, to have phosphorous on your face and feel it eating away right down to the skull. Do you like that picture? Well, that is what your government and mine is doing!

Do you understand what it means to be a sustenance farmer, just growing enough rice for the family to live on for a year? And do you understand how it feels to watch a plane fly overhead spraying chemicals on your field just before harvest, and then watch that field become brown, and then black? Would you like to watch your family starve to death because of some nebulous fight that does not matter? Do you know why it does not matter? Because the very thing that the U. S. seeks to preserve (freedom and abundant life) is that which it destroys every day. Do you understand that bombs and artillery are indiscriminate and don't just cause death and suffering among Vietnamese Communists? Do you understand what it is like to be living in a village in an "insecure" area and to have a plane unload its bombs and then strafe your village without mercy because someone fired at him with a rifle? Can you even begin to imagine the utter horror of being in a village where the planes come in, dropping fragmentation bombs to drive people into the open and then following with napalm and phosphorus bombs to get an effective "kill." My God, can you even imagine what it is like in the villages? Do you know that at least five civilians are killed or wounded for every one combatant in Vietnam?

What does it matter that I work from dawn far into the night trying to increase production so that we can distribute more chicks to the countryside when there is no way to assure the farmer of adequate feed supply, and when a simple quirk of war could wipe him or his family off the face of the earth?

Can you imagine how my Vietnamese friend felt when an American soldier stopped me and asked, in a loud voice, "You aren't a Gook, are you? Don't worry, my friend; we aren't killing persons over here, we are cleaning up the Gooks."

If you could hear me writing this letter you would know that these words are being shouted in desperation and anguish. No, I have never seen the effects of a napalm raid close up, but I am beginning to understand the fear, as I work more out in the villages. I sense the terror that they feel when a flight of jets go overhead. I have seen defoliated fields, and the people who were driven from their homes by the defoliation. Do you understand that almost 90 per cent of the refugees in Vietnam are refugees of U. S. firepower? Have you ever been in a refugee camp? Sensed the hopelessness, the fear, the deep sorrow and yearning for the now destroyed home?

Many of my friends have written and asked if they could help me and my work with an offering of money. I respond to them and to you. If you have been able to grasp even a tiny fraction of the anguish and desperation of this letter, and I have been able to record a fraction of what I feel, and I feel only a fraction of what my people in the countryside feel; then you will do everything in your power and in the power that God offers you to STOP THIS WAR!!! Picket, go to jail, protest, organize politically, preach, pray, write letters, bring our bumbling giant of a nation to its knees. Do whatever is necessary but please, please, in the name of everything that is sane and loving, please STOP THE WAR!

I am sure that there are any number of good reasons why we should be fighting this war, but I really can't find any good enough as I see what this war does to our brethren.

Please don't sleep well tonight, or any night until somehow a way is found to stop destroying human beings in Vietnam.

I send this letter in love and agony.

David Nesmith
IVS/USAID
Advisory Team #3
APO San Francisco
California

What Do You Think?

1.   Is this a true picture of the war? On what did you base your opinion?
2.   What are some good reasons for fighting the war?
3.   The author fails to describe the killing and terrorization by the Viet Cong. Could this letter be considered a description of all modern warfare?
4.   Do you go along with the idea that "all is fair in love and war"?

5.   WORKER DISCONTENT

The image of the teacher as an "obedient" public servant has changed considerably in recent years. If it can be said that students are in revolt, so also are teachers, and, perhaps, for some of the same reasons (such as a growing concern for taking part in the process of determining educational policy). In the following readings, two different writers analyze the reasons for the discontent of teachers, one group of "dirty-workers" (the others being social workers and the police). If "teacher power" becomes a reality, do you think that this will conflict with "student power," or are the interests of the two groups similar?

"The Dirty-Workers Are Striking." *

The dirty-workers are striking—for increased pay, of course, but also for other demands that are more directly related to the dangers of dirty work, and to the disrespect society insists on giving to those who do its tacit bidding. The New York teachers, for example, openly and directly challenged the implicit understanding that it is more important for them to be custodians than for them to be teachers. It is gradually dawning on all of these public servants that both their official public tasks (to educate, to protect the citizens, to look after the welfare of the dependent) and their covert tasks (to control Negroes and make them as invisible as possible) are impossible to achieve.

The dirty-workers are increasingly caught between the silent middle class, which wants them to do the dirty work and keep quiet about it, and

---

* Excerpted from Lee Rainwater, "The Revolt of the Dirty Workers," editorial, *Trans-action,* November 1967. Copyright © 1967 by Washington University, St. Louis Mo. Reprinted by permission from *Trans-action* Magazine.

the objects of that dirty work, who refuse to continue to take it lying down. Individual revolts confront the teachers with the problems of the "blackboard jungle," the police with the problem of "disrespect for law and order," and the welfare workers with the problem of their charges' feigned stupidity and real deception. These civilian colonial armies find their right to respect from their charges challenged at every turn, and often they must carry out their daily duties with fear for their physical safety.

Equally ominous for the dirty-workers is the organized Negro challenge to their legitimacy. Not only must they cope with individual resistance to their ministrations, but also, more and more, with militant and insistent local civil-rights groups that expose their failures and tax them with their abrogation of their professional responsibilities to teach, to protect, to help.

It is encouraging that those expected to do the dirty work are rebelling. But it is really too much to expect that they will admit their own individual culpability, at least as long as the rest of us won't. Even so, the more the teachers, the police, and the welfare workers insist on the impossibility of their tasks, the more that society at large, and its political leaders, will have to confront the fact that our tacit understandings about the dirty work that is to be done are no longer adequate.

Of course there are dangers, too. The police are our internal hawks, and they might win—and there are also hawks among schoolteachers (they want unruly children kicked out of school) and welfare workers (who want to escalate the attack on welfare chiselers). As dangerous in the long run, perhaps, are the doves—the teachers and the social workers who want to save the ghetto through education and casework (or that form of neighborhood casework called "community action"). Should either the ghetto hawks or doves carry the day, their victory could become the basis for a new tacit understanding about dirty work, one that would save the country from paying the price it is apparently most reluctant to pay—the price of providing economic resources and open, decent housing to Negroes, so there is no longer a ghetto that requires dirty-workers.

The Conventional Wisdom *

John Galbraith coins a term in his book *The Affluent Society* which has more than a little application to the teaching profession. Galbraith's term is called the "conventional wisdom" and it refers to the tendency which persons in our society have to avoid that which we obviously can see

---

* Excerpted from Robert E. Phelps, "The Status of the Teacher as an Authority on Instruction," speech reprinted by the California Teachers Association.

to be the reality of a situation and to say those things which people want to hear.

The only refuge from reality in our profession today is to become —in the original Greek sense of the word—an idiot. During the apex of Greek civilization, an idiot could be a highly intelligent, educated, sophisticated person. His erudition could be impressive; his logic compelling; his tastes impeccable. However, if he did not recognize or if he turned away from the relevant issues of his society, he was then an idiot.

I submit to you that, at least in the Greek sense of the word, with regard to the matter which is of more importance to it than any other consideration, the teaching profession has been guilty of being idiotic.

The teaching profession has given lip service to the thought that teaching is the preeminent profession, while in practice most of what we have done has placed the classroom teacher in an inferior and subordinate status. We have said that schools, more than anything else, are for teaching and learning, and yet we have consistently refused to give the classroom teacher the recognition which he deserves as the person and group of persons who is and are the authorities on teaching.

SCHOOL STRUCTURE

[A former] superintendent of schools [in] Jefferson Elementary School District, Daly City, California, pinpoints the problem as follows:

"The ordinary school structure predisposes people, especially those at the teaching level, to feel alienated."

Most school systems are organized in a business-military style, with a hierarchy consisting of the board and the superintendent at the top. The teachers and children are placed in an inferior position at the extreme bottom. This kind of organization inherently reinforces feelings of inadequacy. It encourages indifference and stifles enthusiasm for creative teaching. The alienation is not relieved by salary schedules, merit pay, or sabbatical leaves but remains an integral part of the structure. Unfortunately, changing the structure is no simple matter. It will require a radical realignment of personnel to a more fluid relationship. The concept of hierarchy must go!

Both curriculum development and improvement of instruction are responsibilities of the organized teaching profession. Heretofore, school districts, county offices, the state department of education, and colleges and universities assumed major responsibility for curriculum, sequences of content, and instructional methodology. Teachers have served on curriculum committees in school districts and have conducted studies. They have accomplished some experimentation on teaching methods, but too often not of their own volition, and with limited authority for such experimentation. They were directed more than self-directed.

In short, teachers in the past have been told what to teach, when to teach, and how to teach. Such direction has continued throughout their careers. They have been evaluated on the basis of whether they followed such direction.

What Do You Think?

1. What kinds of conditions might prevent a teacher from teaching?
2. Should teachers have the right to expel unruly students?
3. Should teachers be allowed to strike?
4. How much voice should teachers have in educational policy?
5. What kind of structure might be devised to replace the "hierarchy"?

6.   THE COMPETITIVE GRADING SYSTEM *

Economists who favor a competitive system argue that competition is conducive to efficiency and superior products. How about the competitive system of grades—does the grading system inspire better work?

By present standards of American education, I am a complete and utter success. In 1964 I was class valedictorian at Saint Mary's College High School in Berkeley. During my years at the University of California, Berkeley, I have attained the highest grade-point average of any graduating senior in the College of Letters and Science in the class of 1968.

After 16 years of success, playing the grade-point game, I have come to one overwhelming conclusion: It was not worth it. Now Harvard, Princeton, and Berkeley have all offered me fellowships for graduate study in history. I have turned down their offers and will be doing research at Balliol College, Oxford, this fall. There I shall be evaluated for my work on a personal basis and not by a grading system.

My efforts to win high grades were not worth it for two reasons: Grades got in the way of learning, and the 12 hours a day I spent studying in order to be a success made it almost impossible for me to develop any significant human contacts. My four years of university education, instead of helping me to become a man, have nearly turned me into an unfeeling, unthinking zombie, totally removed from the world outside my own specialized field.

---

* Reprinted from Brian McGuire, "It Wasn't Worth It," *The Saturday Evening Post,* September 21, 1968. Reprinted by permission of Curtis Brown, Ltd. Copyright © 1968 by the Curtis Publishing Company.

A great deal of the fault was my own, for I made the choice to pursue high grades. But the tragic thing is that many educators and most parents uphold the value of high grades as an indication of genuine learning. And American professions and businesses frequently assume that the student who has made high grades is their best potential recruit. Such assumptions exist, I suppose, because it is more convenient to judge a person's ability by number than any other way.

It was foolish of me not to realize that by playing the grade-point game I was compromising my ideals about education and copping out to a dehumanizing system. But the university helped me to fool myself. Its homage to the grade-point standard made it easy for me to assume that because of my grades, I was really learning about the world around me.

In May I gave a speech at a Berkeley Phi Beta Kappa banquet and received a standing ovation for my position against grades. Some people at the university answered my plea for reform by saying that since life is made up of games anyway, one has to learn how to play, and one might as well start at the university. If such is the case, then I think American politicians and educators should stop their platitudes about the greatness of college education, the broadening of the mind, and the development of the individual. The truth, unfortunately, is that most middle-class students attend colleges today because they are under parental or internal pressure to prepare themselves for a well-defined career. Their parents are obsessed with making their way up the socio-economic ladder to the promised land of the "good life," the affluent society with a steak on every grill and three cars in every garage. These parents, and sometimes their children, have equated happiness with the earning power that a college education promises to bring.

But last summer parents all over America found out that their children had stopped believing in this equation. The brightest, most sensitive adolescents from the most well-heeled families began to drop out of society. Thousands of parents began to wonder about the way they had brought up their children. The cute little kids of the early 1950's were suddenly challenging the very homes, education, and society that had so coddled them.

As in our families, so too in our colleges. Abundance is accompanied by despair. The student is surrounded by material things, but he cannot enjoy them because of the void he finds in himself and in the people around him. When I first came to the university at Berkeley in the fall of 1964, I was amazed at the beauty of the place. The buildings, the trees, the huge library, the vast laboratories were all a source of amazement to me.

A few months later, in December, this beautiful image was shattered for me. One morning as I was riding my bicycle up Telegraph Avenue I found the way blocked by paddy wagons taking students to jail. I was upset and confused. I didn't understand what was happening. It was as if for months I had been looking at a beautiful wedding cake and then finally touched it, only to discover that it was made out of cardboard. The arrests were the result of a demonstration by members of the Free Speech Movement. It was the first revolt of the students of the 1960's against the impersonality and alienation that underlie so much of American mass education today. The particular, specific issues were not nearly so important as the feeling on the part of thousands of Berkeley students that the university had lost touch with them as individuals.

I myself did not participate in the Free Speech Movement. I had not yet fully comprehended the game that the university had set up for me to play. Earlier that fall I had told myself that at Berkeley I was not going to worry about grades, that even if I got C's, it would be fine, as long as I was working hard, doing my best, and learning. The important thing, I decided, was to develop myself as a person—physically, mentally, and spiritually. But I soon discarded these high-school ideals. I found that with a great deal of work in the first semester, I was able to earn four A's and one B. After that, the 4.0 symbol (indicating all A's) was far too tempting.

Getting all A's was the best way for me to distinguish myself as a person in the university and to prove to myself that I was really doing what the university expected of me, and I expected of myself. The grade-point symbol became for me the affirmation of my existence, the proof that I was worth something. Subconsciously I knew I was letting the system dominate me and demolish me as an individual. But I could always excuse myself on the grounds that I would need these high grades to get into graduate school.

In America we have become a society of anticipation and anxiety. We are losing meaning, values, and purposes. For many young Americans education means nothing but preparation for a specialized career. Many teachers and students have despaired of asking the great questions and reading the great books. Instead, we have tried to replace belief in values with belief in the so-called scientific method. We still think that those with vast knowledge in a given field, especially one of the sciences, somehow hold the solutions to our personal and social crises. Scientists as scientists cannot be moralists or philosophers or theologians. Nevertheless, many people assume that those who are the most successful specialists in our society can somehow make the most valid generalizations about the ills of America.

I am a case in point. No one would be listening to me now if I were not a specialist in playing the college game of high grades. There are thousands of students all over the country who are tired of struggling for high grades rather than a liberal education. Yet few people have listened seriously to such students because they did not make it to the top of the system. So we tend to dismiss them as lazy or weak. We only listen to the successful in America.

Many Americans, young and old, are lost in their own bags. Those who want to pursue excellence are forced to spend all their time on their work in order to succeed. In the process, they neglect their families and their own personal lives. Those who refuse to acquiesce to the pressure and anxiety of such an existence are often frustrated at their own failure. They feel guilty about their inability to provide their families with as much material affluence as others can. Children in turn see the materialism of their parents and, because of youth's wonderful naiveté, are shocked, disappointed, and angered at the gap between what their parents say about the meaning of life and the way their parents and teachers actually live that life.

School and family reinforce one another. The materialism found at home turns up again in the universities. The preaching is about the higher values of education, but the performance turns out to be training for careers. The teachers themselves, usually fine people, are caught in the bind of taking care of a family, doing research, and teaching. In the great multiversity, teaching usually comes last on the list, for tenure is generally not given for being a good teacher, but for being a successful researcher with a prestigious list of publication credits.

I am not advocating an end to research. Nor am I saying that the technical training college for the engineer or the chemist or the dentist should be dissolved. I am saying that our great multiversities, responsible for educating such a great number of American college students, are going to have to find ways to provide smallness within their bigness. Many worthwhile reforms are possible. All lecture courses could be supplemented with small seminars, run by graduate students who are not overburdened with their own research and study. Professors could be given frequent leaves of absence from their research and paid to concentrate exclusively on teaching. The individual departments within the multiversities, from Anthropology to Zoology, could arrange seminars on educational reform and hold informal meetings at which students and teachers could meet each other on a more personal basis.

All these reforms would be inadequate without a secure structure within the university to provide a basis for intellectual ferment and maturation. I propose the creation of interdisciplinary liberal arts colleges inside the multiversities. These colleges would be open to freshmen and sophomores who wanted to spend the first half of their university education in reading the great books of western civilization. The faculty would be drawn from the various departments of the university and would be expected to abandon or limit their research during their stay in the college. The college faculty and distinguished visitors would give frequent lectures. Every hour of lecture would be matched by an hour of seminar in which students would give their own critiques of the material with which they were dealing. Most seminars would be based on weekly reading assignments, which would cover the primary sources of civilization. Secondary sources, explaining and interpreting the core books, would be optional.

Students would not be expected to become scholars or textual critics. They would be exposing themselves to great literature and history, learning how men think, write, live, and die, so that they might themselves become more aware of their universal situation as human beings. The college would aim at expanding students' minds beyond their immediate cultural milieu. Students would have a chance to see, feel, and appreciate other men, other periods, other life styles, and to relate these experiences and value systems to their own lives. In order to organize their observations and provide some sense of continuity, students would write frequent papers on topics discussed by the teacher and students beforehand. At the end of each semester they would write a few major essays and receive a personal evaluation by their teachers. By the time they reached their junior year and started specializing in majors, students from the interdisciplinary college would be able to think creatively and to deal with relationships between human thought and human experience. Because of their personal contacts within the liberal arts college, they would also feel themselves to be worthwhile, integral parts of a great university instead of cogs in an indifferent machine.

In both the interdisciplinary college and in the traditional university, all grading should be based on personal evaluation. The letter- and the number-grading systems should be replaced by a pass-fail system in all courses except those taken in the student's major field. In that area the student, instead of receiving grades from his professors, would be given individual evaluations by his professors in consultation with his academic supervisor, whom the student himself would choose. The evaluation would not consist of word substitutes for a grade, like "excellent" or "fair," but a comprehensive statement summarizing the student's work and progress and the professor's or graduate student's reaction to that student.

Such a personal evaluation would concede a fact that everyone knows already: Any system of evaluation cannot be completely objective— it is inevitably subject to the bias of the person who is evaluating. Grades should be abolished not because they evaluate, but because they pretend to be objective. It is the lie, the dishonesty, the hypocrisy of the grade-point system that alienates so many students today. It is time we admitted that even professors reading exams are human beings and respond humanly to the people in their courses. Evaluation is ultimately a human act. People cannot fairly evaluate other people by means of numbers or letters.

This mechanical system of evaluation throws light on a much more serious problem. Our universities are not turning out people. They are producing technicians whose feelings and thoughts are forced into mechanical patterns. The big universities are alienating the best of our young people. Administrators, teachers and, most of all, parents and taxpayers do not realize that young people desperately want to understand themselves and the world around them, want to develop ideals and values. Students are as responsible for the alienation as older people, for they often use their idealism as a weapon against their parents and friends instead of accepting these people as they find them. We still approach one another as symbols or ideas. We are still afraid to admit we all are separate individuals who share the same fundamental drives for love and unity.

The big university could transform the rat race by lessening the impersonality of the educational experience. It could well afford to pay more attention to students as people rather than numbers. Our large state universities are favored places where people can come together, learn together, live together, and find out in the microcosm of university life how to be beautiful and dynamic individuals in the macrocosm of the world. They must do this, or they do not deserve to survive.

What Do You Think?

1. Do grades get in the way of learning?
2. What is the difference between "education" and "training"?
3. Are tests a fair way of evaluating what a person knows?
4. What relationship, if any, is there between the giving of grades and dissent?

7.   THE SEARCH FOR MEANING *

In the following article a newspaper columnist reports an interview with a self-described "political" prisoner named Sheila Ryan. Is it possible that there are people like Sheila who may become involved in protest movements, not so much for the protest, but as a way of finding self-identity and meaning in their lives?

Sheila Ryan is 22, with big, Galway-blue eyes, a troubled complexion, and long brown hair that she keeps convent-neat with a big blue ribbon.

---

* Excerpted from John Carmody, "Sheila Ryan, 22, A Political Prisoner," *The Washington Post,* December 8, 1967.

She speaks in a little-girl voice and sits primly with her hands in her lap, her back very straight, as she talks to a visitor at the women's detention center here and says: "I'm not a martyr."

Yet her confederates in the local Students for a Democratic Society (SDS) think she is. They think Sheila Ryan is a political prisoner. The *Washington Free Press*—the local "underground" newspaper that has surfaced far on the new left in recent issues—prints second-hand accounts of her troubles at the detention center.

JAILED

Last August, Sheila Ryan was jailed with six others for 180 days— the maximum sentence for the misdemeanor of illegal entry into a Federal building. The seven had staged a sit-in in the White House in March, 1965, over the Selma, Ala., racial crisis under way at that time. . . .

"I am not a martyr," she says repeatedly. But it is plain that Sheila Ryan does feel caught up in a long, irreversible process—part personally invoked, part historical—that in some deep way satisfies her at the same time it leaves her lonely and alienated in a world she insists she wants to change.

Sometimes, another Sheila Ryan shows through. She says things like "I'd like to be married and have 16 kids."

Or she will grimace and giggle like a young too-far-from-home postulant and say "Oh, God!" when a visitor reminds her that a few years ago she was an all-Massachusetts finalist in the Betty Crocker home-makers contest at Archbishop Williams High School in Braintree. . . .

In her sophomore year [at college] she began working at the receiving home for children on weekends. The middle-class world she had known, as she recalls now, began to crumble then.

"There is nothing so sad," she says, "as to see 8-year-old children in jail—that's what the home really is, you know—who are there because of something done to them—not for what they've done."

Sheila Ryan understands that this was not a unique revelation for a college student. But she took a relatively radical path (although it seems almost commonplace on the campus of 1967) away from what she calls my "schizoid college life."

"It's almost impossible for a middle-class white American to lead a meaningful life today," she says. "But activity is meaningful." For Sheila Ryan that meant the peace and civil rights movements in the already-softening center of the 1965 liberal left.

She answered telephones at the Student Non-Violent Coordinating Committee (SNCC) headquarters here.

She appeared in Cambridge, Md., and before the White House.

"I began to be aware," she says, "When I sat in the White House that time I didn't think about jail. I wasn't aware that maybe I was one of the oppressed—that people who have no control over their lives must be oppressed."

"But later I saw people who only wanted to vote being hit by police with clubs—they had no control over their own lives."

She insists she is not a "straight Marxist." "I am not a complete dialectician. There are really so many different things that can still happen in the world to change things. You can't predict."

But she speaks straight Marx when she talks about "racism and global economics compounded with imperialism—not just American, either"—which demand "a re-allocation of the control of goods and the means of production in this country."

Since she has been in jail, however, Sheila Ryan has steadily narrowed the focus of her protest from symbolic gestures like not washing dishes to the day-by-day conditions of the center. . . .

"Since I've been here," says Sheila Ryan, "I've realized the function of a jail in this society is to control people who don't relate well to oppression. Its function is to put people in total immersion in oppression so they adjust better to the oppression outside again."

She wants to be a "journalist"—although she admits with a smile that "pamphleteer" might be more accurate. On her release from the center in mid-January, she plans to write a series of articles on the jail for the *Free Press.*

MASS

She attends Mass frequently ("lots more than just Sundays") and most of all she waits—as political prisoners—real or imagined—have waited throughout all history and all societies.

Three times a day, seven days a week, the Betty Crocker homemaker finalist washes the dishes of 84 fellow prisoners.

And all the while, the parents in Braintree, Mass., worry. And Sheila Ryan, when the fire dies out in the blue eyes, says she knows they worry. And when the visitor leaves, Sheila Ryan stands behind a jail door and watches through the heavy window until the elevator going down has left again for the world she wants to change.

What Do You Think?

1. Why did the middle-class world crumble for Sheila?
2. What did she mean when she spoke of her college life as "schizoid"?
3. How representative of high school and college students today would you consider Sheila?

8. THE EXPLOITATION OF MINORITIES *

In the central valley of Southern California there has been a long dispute between the grape growers and the grape pickers. Led by Cesar Chavez, the latter group is seeking unionization of all workers as well as protection under legislation that would give workers the benefit of unemployment insurance and other privileges. One unusual aspect of this dispute has been that religious groups have become involved—particularly Roman Catholics—as many of the workers are Mexican and largely of that religion. In the following poem, a Catholic nun gives her reaction to her participation in a march with the grape pickers. Do you think the nun is wrong in taking part in a dispute not involving religious matters?

The Virgin of Guadalupe, the Virgin of Guadalupe
She was on our beautiful banner, and the man,
The farm worker from Delano who carried her,
Led the march. We were going to Modesto.
We were going to show the justice of our cause
A man with a six-foot cross walked behind.

Six miles in two hours, then we stopped
Under the shade of a railway depot
And while we rested we talked.
The people were glad to see us there—
Glad to see the habits of the Church,
I wonder if they know they are the Church?

Young Joey asked if I were tired,
How far we had to go, four miles
I said, and I was tired and Joey said
But we'll walk all those four miles
However tired, for if we sacrifice we win.
This is what the march put into Joey's head.

Then we came to Manteca, and in Manteca,
I learned why the *jefes* spoke so seriously.
I learned what it means to be a minority—
Someone had threatened our lives, and,
The policemen thought we should stay,
Stay in Manteca Park and not march.

---

* Reprinted from Sister Mary Prudence, "The Nun's Tale," *Ramparts,* July 1966.

Cesar Chavez, at night, when we were all together
Asked us to tell why we came to march.
This was our poverty—How could I tell? we had
Only ourselves, only our support to give.
We "Anglos" received much, gave little.
How could I tell him that?

Because we wore the habits of the Church
A farmer offered what he could. No,
We are part of the farm workers, we said,
What you give to us, goes to them.
He knew what the workers needed,
But he was afraid, and we were sorry for him.

"The growers are Catholics," said another
He would not pray, "They can pray for themselves,
They sure don't pray for us."
Cesar Chavez, on Sunday, led a palm procession;
We sang songs in Spanish. Celebrated the Mass.
This is how it was meant to be.

But they are bitter on both sides,
And as we left Manteca, one other man, not with us,
Began to heckle, "Sister, you are ruining
The image of the Church." The image?
And what about the Gospel of the Church? I thought
And what about the duties of the Church, to God's people?

Fresh air and sun and cool water
This is my memory, and burning feet,
Smiles, and the suffering but always
A determination and a hope; this is the beauty
Of it I thought, the beauty in our being here.
Together, we manifest the brotherhood of man.

What Do You Think?

1. Ten years ago a nun would not have even considered going on such a march. How do you account for the change?
2. What did Sister Prudence learn from this march?
3. Of what was the farmer afraid?
4. What is the basic cause for this dissent? Do you think it is just? Why or why not?

ACTIVITIES FOR INVOLVEMENT

1.   There have been many individual voices of dissent in our history, some of them little-known and often given only brief mention in textbooks. For individual or group reports, find further information on any of the dissenters mentioned in Chapter 2, or on the following:
   a. Roger Williams, who was banished from the Massachusetts colony for his "dangerous" ideas, such as suggesting that the religion of the Indians might be just as acceptable to God as Christianity.
   b. Fisher Ames who, although a Federalist, condemned George Washington for using troops to put down the Whiskey Rebellion.
   c. John Brown, whose plan to liberate the slaves by armed intervention led to his death by hanging.
   d. Dorothea Dix, whose belief that the insane should be treated decently led to state laws correcting the evils in asylums.
   e. Henry George, who suggested a single tax on land as a means of eliminating the extremes of poverty and wealth.
   f. Robert Ingersoll, who had very conservative political ideas, but who spoke out for the Darwinian theory and for agnosticism.
   g. Eugene Debs, who went to jail during World War I for speaking against the wartime sedition laws.
   h. Emma Goldman, the anarchist, who was deported to Russia because of her speeches against the capitalist system and authority of the state.
   i. Upton Sinclair, a socialist writer who almost became governor of California.

2.   Although the Supreme Court has ruled on the prayer issue in public schools, Senator Dirksen of Illinois has attempted to overrule that decision by proposing a constitutional amendment. Write for a copy of that proposal, and have a debate on the topic—Resolved: That the Supreme Court should be overruled in the prayer decision. For arguments supporting the Supreme Court decision, write to the nearest chapter of the American Civil Liberties Union. From them you can get many inexpensive pamphlets on a variety of topics.

3.   Write to the Bureau of Indian Affairs in Washington, D. C. for pamphlets on the American Indian. What evidence can you find of dissent by or for Indians in American society?

4.   Invite speakers from minority organizations to speak to your class. Most large cities have chapters of the NAACP or CORE. The American Indian and citizens of Spanish surname also have similar organizations where there is a large concentration of these people.

5.   What is the extent of prejudice and discrimination in your community? Are there segregated schools, housing, churches? Are people denied certain jobs because of race? Plan a series of interviews, by members of the class, with local citizens, members of minority groups, civic leaders, real estate agents, and members of the business community. Also, interview elected officials to determine their feelings about the need for a Fair

Employment Practices Commission, a fair housing law, a Human Relations Commission—if none of these exist.

6.   Review the various causes of dissent presented in the readings in this chapter. Make a list of the various kinds of dissent presented. Now place in rank order from unimportant (at the bottom of the list) to very important (at the top) the various examples. Compare your list with those of your classmates. Be prepared to explain the reasons for ordering the examples as you did.

7.   Look at your list of causes for dissent compiled for Question 6. In what ways are these causes similar? Different? How would you, as an individual, respond to the dissent expressed in each of these readings? Write a brief paper (2–3 pages) in which you attempt to suggest how *one* cause of dissent might be alleviated.

5

Theories About Dissent

In Chapter 2 you read about certain periods of history prior to modern times which were noted for their dissent. Perhaps you have come to some conclusions about the basic reasons why people feel called upon to protest. Are the basic reasons any different now? In Chapter 3 you read many examples of dissenting opinion. Chapter 5 will give you a variety of theories as to *why* there is so much dissent today.

Most of the authors in this chapter are attempting to explain why people today—particularly the young—have become so conspicuous and vocal in their demands. Do these explanations cover the problem adequately?

1. WHY ARE TEENS IN DISSENT? *

The following reading compares the patterns of dissent in contrasting culture areas of the world and illustrates the point that the conformist of one society might be the wild-eyed radical of another. What different factors could account for this?

From Paris to Peking, from London to Singapore, young people are rocking the Establishment boat, upsetting parents, and, in a few cases, threatening to overturn governments. It is a worldwide wave of dissent, and hardly any country has been immune to it.

---

* Excerpted from Sid Goldberg, "From Berkeley to Bangalore—Teens in Dissent," *Senior Scholastic*, April 25, 1968. Abridged and reprinted by permission of Scholastic Magazines, Inc. © 1968 by Scholastic Magazines, Inc.

But one fact stands out in any analysis of youthful dissent around the world: that one man's dissent is another man's conformity. For instance, the long-accepted thing to do in the U. S. is go to religious services on weekends, get married in a religious ceremony, and instill in your children a faith in God. In the Soviet Union, on the other hand, it is a great act of dissent to be a regular churchgoer, and a young man and girl who insist on a church wedding open themselves to the suspicions of the regime and to possible penalties later in life.

Take another example: in Argentina it is an act of open dissent for a young man to wear shoulder-length hair because President Onganía has personally launched a drive against it. Any mop-headed youths encountered by the police are subject to arrest and a haircut by a prison barber (the cueball cut is "in" this year). On the other hand, the worst offense a young Sikh in India can commit against his parents and his religion is to cut his yard-long hair (wrapped under his turban in a braid).

One year's dissent may even be the next year's conformity. Until very recently in Bulgaria all schoolgirls wore black stockings. They were *de rigeur*. But then black stockings became associated with mod Western styles and —presto!—black stockings were banned in Bulgarian schools. Today, if a schoolgirl in Sofia wants to get called in to the principal's office for a scolding and possible punishment, all she need do is put on black stockings.

Another point about youthful dissent around the world: while dissent in the democracies can sometimes be trivial, ludicrous, or downright pointless, virtually any dissent in a dictatorship must be heroic. In the U. S., particularly, most young people enjoy great freedom of expression. To challenge the truth of this, it is sometimes necessary to go to absurd lengths—such as the so-called Filthy Speech Movement launched by a few students at the University of California in Berkeley [some] . . . years ago.

While a few American students may still think the right to say dirty words in public is worth devoting their time to, thousands of students in Poland have recently taken to the streets over a free-speech issue that most Americans take for granted—the right to express "non-official" opinions. Behind the Polish protest: the closing of a classic Polish play, *Dziady (Forefathers),* written more than a hundred years ago by Poland's greatest poet, Adam Mickiewicz. The Communist authorities objected when audiences cheered at some anti-Russian lines in the play.

Throughout the Soviet Union itself, the young generation is also in ferment over the free speech issue. It reached a boiling point this past year with the imprisonment of two of the Soviet Union's most talented young writers, Yuli Daniel and Andrei Sinyavsky, for allowing works critical of the U. S. S. R. to be published abroad. Since then, one young writer after another has stepped forward in defense of Daniel and Sinyavshy, each thereby putting his own career and freedom on the block.

One of them was Yuri Galanskov, who wrote an open letter to Mikhail Sholokhov, who represents the Soviet literary Establishment (and who won a Nobel Prize for literature for books like *And Quiet Flows the Don*). Galanskov, who since has been arrested and now languishes in a Soviet prison, wrote to Sholokhov:

> In any other country, where basic democratic freedoms are actually upheld and not merely paid lip service, people would have demanded the release of the accused (Daniel and Sinyavsky) and they would have protested the government's action openly. Had the case occurred in a democratic society, a number of literary figures would have left the Union of Soviet Writers in protest, and maybe established a rival union, for instance a Union of Russian Writers. But in our country the people who wrote plaintive letters for permission to defend freedom and justice did so as though they were swindlers. So far this is still the protest of slaves, but it is a protest nevertheless."

Even in Communist China, student dissent is a factor that has to be dealt with. Some observers say that one reason behind Mao Tse-tung's Cultural Revolution was the fear that youthful energies, unless channeled in other directions, might be directed against the regime itself. And so Mao and his Peking aides shut down the entire school system of Communist China for one year, during which time the young Red Guards were invited to let off steam. They were allowed to roam through China, beating up alleged "reactionaries" and "anti-Maoists." Whether Mao can shut off or redirect this youthful energy as quickly as he turned it on still remains to be seen.

What's behind this student uproar all over the world? Is dissent in itself a good thing? The second question is easier to answer than the first. The mere act of dissenting is neither good nor bad. If the conforming majority agrees that two plus two is four and the nonconformist student insists it is five, most would agree that he doesn't deserve any credit for his dissenting view. But if the "Establishment" insists that such-and-such is correct or honorable, and the dissenters won't go along with either the logic or the viewpoint, then the picture changes. Or to look at it from another angle: In the first years of the 1930's, the most "involved" students in Germany, then a tottering democratic republic, were the young Nazis. They shouted down teachers they disapproved of, tossed anti-Nazi professors out of windows, and beat up other students who ridiculed Adolf Hitler. Certainly these young Nazi dissenters don't win our admiration.

Dissent is to be admired or scorned depending on the issues involved. The chief problem today is that sometimes the younger and older generations disagree on the very meaning of the issues.

As to what's behind it, one of the first factors to be considered is that there are so many students in the world today. In India alone there are 70 million. Whereas 50 years ago high school and college were available to only a tiny percentage of the world's youth, today they are available to millions—so the student segment of society is a force that can make itself be heard and reckoned with.

Because of mass education, there is greater awareness among youth. The Brazilian youth, who a generation ago might be helping his father eke out a living from his coffee crop, today goes to high school and learns of a whole new world—in which there are many other alternatives to peasant farming. He begins to wonder whether perhaps his father's way of life isn't wrong, and whether it should be changed. And in the exuberance of youth, changes must be made quickly—right now.

And of course there has developed an entire new psychology of child-rearing in this century. Not so many years ago, the theory was that "children should be seen and not heard," that they should merely listen to the wisdom of their elders. Today the theory is that children should be encouraged to express themselves from the earliest age. Parents, as a whole, have become more permissive than in earlier generations. And by the time their offspring are ready for college, their dissenting views come across loud and clear—too loud and clear for the likes of some.

Of course, the vast majority of high school and college students, especially in the U. S. and the Western democracies, believe that dissent should be expressed entirely within the framework of the democratic process. That means if you don't like the way things are being done in this country, speak up and argue peacefully for a different way—the key word being "peacefully." If enough people think the same way as you do, then your views will have the sanction of the majority and be put into effect. This, ironically, is precisely the goal that so many student dissenters in dictatorships are still pressing for.

What Do You Think?

1.   For what reasons are young people in dissent around the world today?

2.   How would you explain the fact that a conformist in one society might often be considered a radical in another society?

2. ALIENATION *

The "multiversity" has grown to such size that many students feel lost in the bureaucracy of such an institution. Is it size alone that creates such a situation, or are there other factors which add to the impersonalization process? How does such impersonalization contribute to dissent?

When the king of Bavaria was informed on Nov. 9, 1918, that revolution had deprived him of his throne, he is supposed to have replied, "But are they allowed to do that?"

How many members of the "establishment" have responded to recent student revolts with similar expressions of shocked disbelief? No doubt, students are not "allowed" to occupy university buildings, destroy university property, and to bring the business of the university to a standstill. But they are doing it all over the world.

Nothing is simpler than to counter this particular manifestation of the world revolution of the students with the invocation of "law and order" and the call for the police. But nothing is less appropriate and more self-defeating, for a university administration which is reduced to calling the police thereby admits its defeat.

A couple of hundred determined students are capable of administering that defeat to any university administration. It is this extreme vulnerability of the university which makes it incumbent upon the administration to take preventive action forestalling that student violence which calls forth the violence of the police.

Instead of being concerned with the maintenance of "law and order" per se, such action must be informed by the issues from which the student revolts have arisen. Some of these issues are of universal significance and philosophic or even spiritual in nature; others arise from a particular political situation.

What the students revolt against in their universities is what they are revolting against in the world at large. That world, thoroughly secularized and dedicated to the production of consumer goods and weapons of mass destruction, has lost its meaning.

What does a man live for? What is his purpose in life? What is the meaning of death, which appears to wipe out that life as though it had never existed?

Young men have always asked such questions; in times past they

---

* From Hans J. Morgenthau, "But Are They Allowed to Do That?", *The Christian Science Monitor,* July 19, 1968.

went to their priest, minister, or rabbi to get an answer. Now they go to the university, which, they have been told, is dedicated to the search for truth about man, society, and the universe.

But those are not the questions universities raise, let alone answer. Rather, to paraphrase what Tolstoy said about historiography, they try to answer questions nobody has asked and which in any event are as meaningless to the student as is the world in which he lives.

That world is also thoroughly mechanized and bureaucratized. Thus it diminishes the individual, who must rely upon others rather than himself for the satisfaction of his wants, from the necessities of life to his spiritual and philosophic longings. The modern university is a microscopic replica of that world. The modern university has become a soulless, computerized machine which processes degreeless students for the purpose of making them comply with the requirements of an academic degree.

STUDENTS DOUBLY PROVOKED

By assuming functions *in loco parentis* [1] it provokes its students in a dual way:

· It invokes parental care by assuming these functions, which hardly a modern parent is able to perform.

· And by trying to perform these functions (which once sprang from the parental love of kin) in the only manner it is capable of (that is the unpersonal, mechanical, bureaucratic one) it denigrates in the minds of the students the memory of parental love and gives a lie to its own pretenses.

The modern university, then, has become irrelevant to the aspirations of its students. By putting forth a claim—the disinterested search for the truth—it does not live up to, it is judged by its students to be hypocritical, if not dishonest, as well.

But if the modern university does not raise the questions to which the students want an answer, it raises an abundance of questions posed by interested parties in business and government.

The modern university has become a gigantic service institution, fed massively by corporate and government funds. It does not sit in judgment over society and government in the Socratic or prophetic manner, but it gives indiscriminate service on a cost-plus fee basis.

The modern university has become so intimately involved in the affairs of society and government that it appears to the students as an agent of society and government. What they find wrong with, and oppose, in the latter, they find objectionable in the former.

---

[1] In the place of a parent

GRIEVANCES FOCUS ON UNIVERSITY

In other words, those accumulated grievances against society and government which the students harbor are released against that institution of which the student is supposed to be a part and which is physically accessible to him. The university becomes the scapegoat for his spiritual, philosophic, and political frustrations.

These frustrations are nourished by three basic experiences:

· First, the individual experiences his diminution as a person (to which I have referred before) in a particularly acute way when he operates in the political sphere; for the domination of man by man is the distinguishing characteristic of that sphere. He feels insignificant and helpless in the face of the powers-that-be. He cannot protect himself against them.

· And—this is the second source of political frustration—he appears not to be able to influence them. Students have demonstrated for freedom of speech in totalitarian countries; they have demonstrated against the Vietnam War and in support of racial justice in the United States and elsewhere. But so far what has been the result of all these demonstrations? Totalitarian governments still allow freedom of speech only to the rulers, the Vietnam War is still going on, and racial justice is still a postulate rather than a fact.

The powers-that-be appear to be impervious to pressures from below. Attempts at reforming the system from within appear to be futile. There appears to be nothing left but to oppose the system itself.

· This experience of futility is powerfully reinforced and made definitive by a third factor; the lack of a viable alternative to the dominant philosophy, regime, and policies. That is as true of the Soviet Union as it is of West Germany, of Japan as it is of the United States. What difference does it make for whom one votes when the policies of different persons and parties are virtually interchangeable?

In the United States, these universal factors have taken on a peculiar poignance because of the Vietnam War and the racial crisis. On the Vietnam War the powers-that-be have first deluded themselves, and then they have deceived the people. On the racial issue, the government has aroused expectations it could not live up to.

Faced with these multiple obstacles, a passionate longing for radical change found, not surprisingly, an outlet in violence. That resort to violence was rendered virtually inevitable for those who resorted to it, lacking a viable program for change.

"Participatory democracy" is a slogan which points to the deficiencies of the present system; it gives no inkling as to how the system can be changed and the individual can be made whole in the contemporary world. What we have here is a revolt against the status quo on behalf not of a coherent political philosophy or program but rather of an amorphous longing for liberation, for meaning, for salvation.

THREE STEPS RECOMMENDED

The modern university has no way of satisfying this longing. But it can at least avoid the appearance of standing in the way of its satisfaction and of mocking it.

Three courses of action could serve these ends:

First, the university can decentralize its administrative structure and thereby make it possible for the student to participate in the life of the university on a basis of at least approximate equality.

Second, the university can try to recover its independence by ceasing to identify itself completely with the status quo of government and society.

Finally and most importantly, the university can again ask the fundamental questions about man, society, and the universe—for the sake of which it was originally established.

Regardless of what it does or does not do, the modern university cannot escape a dilemma:

On the one hand, it must maintain certain standards, without which, to paraphrase Kant, there would be no point in having universities.

On the other hand, it is defenseless against the violence of a couple of hundred of its members who will destroy these standards.

Yet while it cannot escape that dilemma, it can blunt the sharp edges of the dilemma's second horn.

Thus the best it can do is to minimize the likelihood of violence. But considering the malaise of which violence is a mere symptom, it cannot escape its threat.

What Do You Think?

1. It has been said that the function of the school is "to train the mind." Does this agree with any of the statements made by the writer, or does it contradict his statement? Which statements?

2. What "questions" do the young people of today want answered?

3. Review the ideas expressed in Reading 2 in Chapter 3. In what ways are they similar to the ideas expressed in this reading? Different?

4. Does political control of a university affect its function as an institution of learning? Explain. Does such control contribute to student dissent?

5. Would decentralization help to decrease student dissent? Why or why not?

3. THE DOCTRINE OF PERMISSIVENESS *

Are parents and schools too easy on the youth of today? In this reading, Dr. Max Rafferty, the State Superintendent of Public Instruction in California, and a candidate for the Senate of the United States in 1968, argues that "the cult of the slob" has taken over in this country. Would there be a connection between such a cult and dissent?

Let's get one thing straight. This country has just as large a percentage of decent, law-abiding youngsters as it ever had. But the minority who always got into trouble in the past are getting into worse trouble now. Their crimes are more sordid; their attitude is more defiant; their contempt for moral and legal codes is more outspoken.

Why? Well, for one thing, the doctrine of permissiveness which was just another name for "the easy way out" took over both the homes and the schools about two decades ago, and produced the least repressed child. Junior played with his toys but refused to put them away, threw the spinach on the dining room floor but got the ice cream anyway, sassed his parents and his teachers to their faces and got away with it. As a teenager, Junior stole the old man's whiskey and shared it with the gang, drag-raced on the county highway at midnight with the family car, and told both the cop and the judge to go to hell when he was finally hauled in. He feared nothing and respected nobody because he had never been compelled at an early age to do either. The behavioristic psychologists and their allies the progressive educationists were right about one thing: they have managed to turn out a large number of young people with remarkably few repressions. Repressions, in fact, are in extremely short supply these days. Witness our books, our drama, our motion pictures. We could use more repressions, I think—a lot more.

Almost a decade ago, I wrote a little piece for a national magazine called the "The Cult of the Slob." In it, I tried to draw a picture of the future:

He stands before us, unwashed and unregenerate. His hair is long and kneaded behind into strange whorls and sinuosities. Below the ears and following the slack jawline, it descends in bristling tufts, and with an exuberance unknown since the more militant days of the late General Burnside. Hairiness is, in fact, the very badge and

* Excerpted from Dr. Max Rafferty, "The Meaning of Berkeley," copyright 1966, *Los Angeles Times*.

symbol of the Slob. He spends a considerable portion of his day coiling and matting, as the Mock Turtle did reeling and writhing.

His stance approximates the so-called debutante slouch of a generation ago. His walk is an exaggerated, hip-swinging roll which harks back to the gait of the old saltwater sailor temporarily marooned on land. His talk is a modern thieves' jargon, relying strongly upon scarcely disguised obscenity and intelligible mainly to other members of the cult. His music is the monotonous and nerve-wracking drum-beat of the primeval jungle.

Slobbism negates all the values which we teach. It convulses hysterically against all discipline. It derides morality in any form. It persistently seeks out ugliness and filth in preference to beauty and decency, like the unlovely but irreproachable Biblical dog which insisted on returning to its own vomit.

What Do You Think?

1.   What limits to freedom should parents or schools set?
2.   Would you agree that there is a breakdown in morality in the teenager of today? Why or why not?
3.   Has the "doctrine of permissiveness" increased in this country?
4.   Dr. Rafferty states that we could "use more repressions, I think—a lot more." What does he mean by this? Would you agree? Why or why not?

4.   THE HIPPIES: CREATIVE DROPOUTS OR ESCAPIST COPOUTS? *

The motives for human behavior are often complex and defy a simple explanation. Does the following selection give any clue as to why some people dissent?

Lisa described group living as a learning arrangement where "we all help each other. What we're learning is how to play games, to un-learn all the things we've been taught. It's a sort of ego loss."

"Ego loss! It's all phony," broke in Ron Thelin, formerly co-owner of the Psychedelic Shop. Ron, a thin, bearded, red-haired youth who speaks in an intense monotone, put it this way: "The hippies haven't

---

* Excerpted from Anne Henehan, "The Hippies: Creative Dropouts or Escapist Copouts?", *Senior Scholastic,* November 16, 1967. Abridged and reprinted by permission of Scholastic Magazines, Inc. © 1967 by Scholastic Magazines, Inc.

lost ego. They're just like everybody else." He raised his eyes from the flowers he was arranging behind the counter of the shop. "These poor kids—what they don't know is that no chemistry, no drugs, no LSD is going to make people beautiful, any more than any cosmetic would.

I had hoped to see a Renaissance, with people all living honestly. Instead, we just have a lot of sick kids dependent on drugs—the way middle-class society is dependent on money and alcohol. Middle-class society is a lot sicker, but the hippies are sick too!"

One Hashbury hippie, who goes by the name Teddybear, put it this way to a reporter for the *Washington Post:* "There never were any flower children. This wasn't a 'Summer of Love,' this was a summer of bull and you, the press, did it. The so-called flower children came here to find something because you told 'em to, and there was nothing to find.

"They got all the rules written down, how to dress, how to behave, what to say. They only had to turn on their television sets or open a magazine or a newspaper and read: 'Come to San Francisco, the City of Saint Francis, with a flower in your hair.' You told 'em to come here and everything would be free, free crash pads, free food, free dope. The only things I got free was from my friends. Truthfully this community is based on dope, not love."

It is the hippies' extensive use of drugs—especially marijuana and LSD, and in some cases even stronger drugs—which puts off many outsiders who might otherwise sympathize with some hippie ideas. "Why can't most hippies develop their own creativity and form purposeful relationships without using drugs as a crutch?" is the key question many are asking. "Why is it," they go on, "that hippies have substituted drug-produced fantasies for positive moral values? Doesn't the hippies' escape from facing up like mature men and women to what others before them have faced up to with more courage?"

The hippies and their defenders reply that the movement is much involved with social problems. "You say the hippies are not concerned with politics," argues one defender, "only because you have such a narrow concept of what politics is."

A random sampling of Haight-Ashbury residents found that most of them did feel strongly about political issues in which they thought there was a moral issue involved—such as the Viet Nam War.

But most others simply sat on the sidewalk, playing their oboes or guitars. Some stood on street corners, gossiping, or hawking underground newspapers to goggle-eyed tourists. Some sat in makeshift, storefront "temples," meditating with the obvious stimulus of marijuana or LSD. Others ran souvenir shops, psychedelic poster shops, or pornograph book stands, apparently at a big profit.

It seemed, to an outsider, that "Hashbury," and probably all of hippiedom, was a microcosm of the "straight" world. Its denizens were by no means all alike. There were the leaders and the joiners, the kids for kicks and the true believers in some sort of spiritual cause. There were searchers and escapists. There were those sincerely concerned about their fellow men, and those who weren't averse to making money from them. And there were some who were just "losers," who couldn't have made it anywhere.

The hippies kept saying they had not so much dropped out of organized society as organized a society of their own. It seemed, to them, a Brave New World right now. But I could not help but feel that, in time, it would probably develop all the hang-ups and tensions of "straight" society, and become something else to drop out of. . . .

What Do You Think?

1. Do you think the hippies will improve society by dropping out of it? Explain your reasoning.
2. Would you support the type of program which the hippies seem to offer? Why or why not?
3. Would you consider the hippies as "true" dissenters or rather exhibitionists? Explain.

5.   REVOLUTION FOR THE SAKE OF REVOLUTION *

Why do young people join revolutionary causes? Is it just for kicks? Or are they serious in wanting to reform society?

New York—When violent student rebellions erupted all over America and Europe last spring, I was naive enough to go along with a commonly-held liberal view that they were largely a spontaneous manifestation of youthful discontent.

Some kind of social phenomenon, it seemed, was responsible for the cataclysm of action whose fronts involved not only great American campuses and barricades in Paris but also Spain, Italy, England, Germany, Belgium, Sweden, Poland, Czechoslovakia, and Yugoslavia.

What made the argument for spontaneity credible was the fact that the revolutionary explosion had no discernible political orientation. The youthful rebels were raising similar hell whether their worlds were Democratic, Communist, or Fascist.

Their target, wherever it was located, was the Establishment—and thus what was happening appeared to be a magnified, more violent but natural nuclear-age version of youth's perennial challenge to their elders.

---

* Excerpted from William Randolph Hearst, "Revolution for the Hell of It," *San Francisco Examiner-Chronicle,* September 22, 1968.

Well, that's just what it was, but with a single, all-important exception. Far from being natural and spontaneous, the hell-raising was the calculated result of long planning.

The planners, or, rather, plotters, are the leaders of a comparatively-new world revolutionary movement. Mostly young, they seek nothing less than the total destruction of all existing government order everywhere.

Their heroes are Mao Tse-tung and Che Guevara, although they themselves are not Communists. Communism is too tame for them.

Instead, by their own boastful admission, they are unalloyed anarchists.

They are revolutionaries just for the hell of it.

*   *   *   *   *

[T]he hell-raising is going to continue, not only in the United States, but all over Europe.

The culprits are a comparatively small number of world-organized young anarchists who have not the slightest idea of what they would do if their crazy dreams of total disorder were to come true.

Unlike most revolutionaries of the past, they have no plans whatever for a better society.

To the best of my knowledge, they have never suggested economic, political, or social substitutes of any kind.

By no means do they represent—or speak for—the huge majority of today's serious, idealistic, and educational-seeking youth. They are, in fact, giving their generation an undeserved bad name.

All the troublemakers represent is rebellion for the sake of sheer disruption and destruction.

What Do You Think?

1. Is there a hard core of troublemakers today who represent "rebellion for the sake of sheer disruption and destruction"?
2. How might a hippie respond to the argument above?

6. THE GENERAL AFFLUENCE *

Are college students of today a spoiled generation who unconsciously rebel because of deep-seated guilt feelings about their own affluence? How about you—do you detach yourself from the suffering of others, or do you suffer with them?

---

* Excerpted from Lewis B. Mayhew, "Changing the Balance of Power," *Saturday Review,* August 17, 1968. Copyright Saturday Review, Inc., 1968.

There are, of course, a number of other hypotheses as to why students, especially the restless or militant ones, seek confrontations. These range from the influence of permissive parents to the impersonality of life in a complex world, and from the impact of affluence to the disillusionment that comes when faith in the perfectibility of man is challenged by reality.

At least two other factors clearly play a role, however. The first is the general affluence of middle-class white America, existing as it does beside a tradition rooted in Calvinism and the rejection of pleasure. Somehow, both adults and students in American colleges display considerable guilt over "never having had it so good." Restless students opt for the poverty of the dropout; faculty opt for extending the work day and week into times once reserved for recreation. Somehow the student who can wear old clothes, eat simple fare, and scorn the "fat cats" can ease the guilt that comes from knowing he has had a life of luxury. Equally, the professor who flies at night to avoid a day of work and who carries his "own" work into the weekends is coping with similar feelings.

This problem of affluence is intensified by the plight of minority groups in America and by the war in Vietnam. There is more than a suspicion that at least part of our present affluence is war-based. Hence to enjoy affluence is to condone a war the justice of which is in considerable doubt. The protesting college student may well be compensating for his knowledge that if a war-based economy had not made his parents affluent he might be fighting the war instead of attending college. Police billy clubs are still safer than Vietcong grenades, and he knows it.

The moral dilemma of affluent America over the plight of the Negro is, of course, the most divisive force in society. The guilt and grief with which white America mourned the death of Martin Luther King is illustrative of the subterranean feeling there before his death. It is no accident that the student protest derived from the civil rights movement. When that movement ceased to welcome white students, other protest activity was used to sublimate the guilt of more than three hundred years of injustice.

What Do You Think?

1. How is class (lower, middle, upper) determined in our society? Does class have anything to do with attitudes or ways of thinking? With dissent?

2. Are many middle-class students today guilty over "never having had it so good"? Why might this be so?

ACTIVITIES FOR INVOLVEMENT

1.   Take a poll of the class on the following:
   a. Is dissent the same as disagreement?
   b. Is dissent good for our society?
   c. Under what conditions might it be considered as not being good?
   d. Is the dissenter justified in resorting to civil disobedience? To violence?
   e. Is there more dissent today than in the past?

2.   Write a short paper on the topic: Resolved: That civil disobedience can be justified as a legitimate means to bring about social improvement. Then hold a class discussion as to why various students feel as they do.

3.   Review the various explanations for dissent discussed in this chapter. Compare these explanations with the causes of dissent you listed after reading Chapter 3. (Recall your answer to Question 6 following Chapter 3.) What types of dissent are not covered by these explanations?

4.   The readings in this chapter discussed why certain individuals or groups engaged in dissent. As a class activity, take a poll (in writing) of each student in the class, having him give his opinion of the explanation of dissent in each of the following cases:
   a. The hippies.
   b. High school students.
   c. Minorities.
   d. Women.
   e. The "New Left" (SDS).
   f. Right wing groups (such as the supporters of George Wallace).
   g. Farm workers.
   h. College students.
Tabulate the results, and discuss the reasons for the different replies.

5.   The civil-rights movement today is conducted mainly by blacks, but several other minorities such as the American Indian and people of Spanish surname have joined the protest. Earlier in our history, immigrant groups were the "outsiders" and suffered varying degrees of discrimination before being accepted and assimilated into the mainstream of American life.

   Divide the class into groups to gather data on several such peoples: The Irish, the Jews, the Chinese, the Italians, the Poles—to name a few examples. Have the investigators present this data to the class in a panel presentation. In looking up information about each group, consider the following points as guidelines:
   a. Why did they come to America?
   b. What problems did they face after arriving?
   c. If they were the victims of prejudice, and the prejudice led to discrimination, did it happen because of:
      · bigotry (religious prejudice)?
      · economic reasons (competition for jobs)?
      · social factors (skin color, strange customs or dress, poverty, etc.)?
      · a combination of the above?

d. If they were eventually assimilated, how and why did this happen?

e. Is there any basis of comparison between your group and a minority seeking equality today? If, for instance, your group was assimilated, how do you explain the fact that others have not been fully accepted as "Americans"?

f. Is there any basis for comparison between these minorities and student groups seeking "student power"? Explain.

(Note: Consult the bibliography for suggested sources of information.)

6

Reactions
to Dissent

What is the effect of dissent on our society? Some people react with indifference, others with mild disapproval, and still others with an emotionalism that may even include violence. Is the generation gap of significance here? Are most older people conformists who resist change, in contrast to young persons who are receptive to new ideas? The readings in this chapter will give you some examples of the different kinds of reactions that dissent produces.

1. "KILL HER, HIT HER HARDER." *

One of the easiest ways to react to dissent is through pure, unadulterated hate. Here is one example of what hatred can bring to those who dissent.

After provoking widespread wrath with her winning fight to abolish school prayer, Madalyn Murray is now out to uproot religion altogether by taxing the nation's churches out of existence.

"You atheist, you mongrel, you rat, Jesus will fix you, you scum."

Angrily she stalked the room, disarrayed, coarse of manner, broad of gesture, masculine of voice, saying, "If people want to go to church and be crazy fools, that's their business. But I don't want them praying in ball parks, legislatures, courts, and schools. I don't want to see their religion

---

* Excerpted from Robert A. Liston, "Mrs. Murray's War on God," *The Saturday Evening Post,* July 11, 1964. Reprinted by permission of Curtis Brown, Ltd. Copyright © 1964 by the Curtis Publishing Company.

emblazoned on the public buildings I look at. They can believe in their virgin birth and the rest of their mumbo jumbo, as long as they don't interfere with me, my children, my home, my job, my money, or my intellectual views."

These words were spoken vehemently to me by Mrs. Madalyn Murray of Baltimore, the nation's most militant atheist, who has declared war on God and the Church and hopes to destroy both. Thanks to her unrelenting pugnacity, a good part of society has declared war on Mrs. Murray. Not long after our interview, she was hauled into court by the Baltimore police and charged with assault for engaging in a scuffle with cops outside her home. The fight flared when police tried to take into custody a 17-year-old girl to whom Mrs. Murray gave shelter after the girl had fled her own home. Charging that Mrs. Murray had turned the runaway's head with atheistic ideas, the girl's parents sought legal help to get her back. As Mrs. Murray later described the incident, a crowd of "at least 250 people" formed to watch her struggle with the cops. The crowd, she said, bawled, "Kill her, hit her harder." She collapsed and had to be carted to the hospital before going to court. Released on bail, she promptly gathered up her family and hopped a plane for Hawaii, declaring that she feared for her life in Baltimore. She vowed to carry on from Hawaii her unyielding war on the Almighty. She might be dismissed as a crank, except that she has already won the first battle in her war—abolition of religious exercises in public schools. Immediately, she launched the next assault. She is now seeking to eliminate the churches' exemption from property taxes. She wants to compel churches to pay income, sales, excise, entertainment, and other taxes, and she hopes to do away with individual income-tax deductions for church contributions. Ultimately, she wants to wipe out every manifestation of Godliness in American life.

The financial burden she wants to lay on churches would be staggering. Mrs. Murray estimates that in one year churches would pay taxes to city, state, and federal governments equal to the national debt. But no one knows for sure. Churches have never been taxed, and accurate appraisals of their net worth and income have never been made. Isolated studies vary widely in their results. One survey indicates that churches may own two to five per cent of all taxable property, and that real-estate tax revenues might increase three to six per cent if churches were taxed. Another study says that churches own 14 per cent of all taxable property in Pennsylvania, 17 per cent in Maryland, and 18 per cent in New Jersey. A third study estimates the Catholic Church owns tax-exempt property in the United States worth $11 billion, including 38 per cent of the tax-exempt property in Washington, D. C.

In these figures, Mrs. Murray thinks she sees the way to overthrow religion in this country. Believing the power to tax is the power to destroy, she prophesies, "If churches have to pay taxes like everyone else, they will wither away and die within thirty to forty years."

That is her aim, and she states it repeatedly: "I want to be able to walk down any street in America and not see a cross or any other sign of religion. I won't stop till the Pope—or whoever the highest religious authority is—says Atheists have a right to breathe in this world."

Mrs. Murray is far from alone in her efforts. She has formed an organization called the Freethought Society, which has a secret membership, dues and directors, publishes a magazine, has a national headquarters at 2502 North Calvert Street in Baltimore—and has gathered a $40,000 war chest to fight the tax-exemption cases [all the way] to the Supreme Court.

Paradoxically Mrs. Murray also has indirect support from religious quarters. A proposed Constitutional amendment to undo the ban on school prayer has been opposed in testimony before a Congressional committee by nearly all Jews and by the National Council of Churches, which represents most Protestants in this country. Furthermore, there are clergymen who openly advocate taxation of churches. The Rev. Dr. Eugene Carson Blake, stated clerk (chief administrative officer) of the United Presbyterian Church and past president of the National Council of Churches, has written: "The economic power that will be increasingly wielded by ever richer churches threatens to produce not only envy, hatred, or resentment of nonmembers but also to distort the purposes of the church members and leaders themselves . . ." He prophesies "that with reasonably prudent management, the churches ought to be able to control the whole economy of the nation within the predictable future."

If this happens, it will be over the dead body of Madalyn Murray, a strange, immensely complicated woman, full of paradoxes, conflicts, and challenges. She is a woman who can in one moment be loud, profane, vain, arrogant, seemingly paranoid, messianic, rebellious, and implausible in her ideas, and in the next be gentle, intelligent, reasonable, thought-provoking, and monumentally courageous.

"You're right," she said to me during an interview, "I don't really care that much about atheism. I'm not well-read in philosophy and theology. I've always been more interested in politics and social reform. But I've gotten into this thing, and I've been driven out of the community. Atheism is all I have to fight my way back in with. I want respect for my right to have any opinion I want—and to live. I could be a damned fascist and do the same thing I'm doing now."

How did she become an atheist? "I read the Bible one weekend when I was thirteen," she says, "the whole way through. I'll never forget the shock of it. The improbability of it was just too much, and the miracles would stop anybody. I kept wondering how anyone could believe the thing. Later I did more formal studies, and the Bible remained unbelievable. The Old Testament is full of cruelty, sadism, and hatred, and the New is much too mystical. The miracles are too wild and counter to all experience. If I had heard of, or there was any scientific possibility of, virgin birth or walking on water, I might be able to start to accept it. But there isn't.

"And what good is it as a normal influence? Christianity has been around 2,000 years, and we are no more moral now than before. If anything, we are more beastly. Would the Greeks have killed six million Jews? Would the Romans have dropped an A-bomb on a city largely populated with women and children? Personal morality has suffered too. Just look at the crime statistics."

Mrs. Murray wrote the school board asking that Bill [her son] be allowed to leave the room during the five-minute Scripture reading and the Lord's Prayer recitation at Woodburne Junior High School, where he was an eighth-grader. If this was not done, she said, she would take him out of school. Dr. George B. Brain, the school superintendent, informed Mrs. Murray that school prayers were in accordance with a 1911 rule of the Board of Education, that the rule had never been challenged and that Bill could not be excused. If he did not wish to participate, he could remain in his seat in respectful silence.

On October 12, 1960, Mrs. Murray took her son out of school and did not return him until October 28, when the board agreed to restudy its prayer ruling. Later the board reversed Doctor Brain, deciding non-believers could leave the classroom during religious exercises. But Mrs. Murray had already decided to challenge the constitutionality of school prayers. Her court case, Murray vs. Curlett (the board president), went to the Supreme Court, where she won.

"My youngest son has been stoned. A nine-year-old boy stoned by Christians! But the worst was when he was six. The teacher told him about hell and purgatory. He runs home bawling. 'I'm going to be burned up. Jesus Christ died for me, Why? I didn't mean to kill anybody.'

"Let me tell you what my Christian neighbors have done. Every window has been broken at least once. We've been rotten-egged. Trees have been broken off, roses stepped on. They've brought their dogs to urinate on my pansies—a free-thought symbol. For us to have a little beauty in our home, to somehow live normally, is something my neighbors cannot stand.

"Our automobile has been vandalized time and again. Windows have been broken, tires slashed. There's even been a bullet through the side. Repair bills have run as high as $600.

"Do you know what somebody did? I went to the hospital for several major operations. At my lowest point I was in the recovery room being fed intravenously. Somebody called up anonymously with a phony report my father had died. They hoped the shock of it would kill me. Well, I'm a pretty hard nut to crack.

"Let me tell you how my father did die. It was about Christmas time in 1962. We celebrate Christmas at our house with a tree and outdoor decorations. There were repeated raids. Our decorations were stolen. Outdoor electric sockets were shorted out. The boys' sleds were stolen. Then in January a bunch of hellions walked all over the top of Dad's car. I caught them and planned to take them to court. My father, who had a bad heart, said, 'You cannot go into court anymore. I cannot stand it. This will kill me.' So I wrote to the parents of each boy suggesting they punish them. But the harassment had been too much. A few days later Dad died of a heart attack.

"He was a Presbyterian, and we had a church funeral. Know what? We couldn't get enough pallbearers to carry him out. And at the funeral the preacher tried to convert me and see if he couldn't get prayers back into schools."

Mrs. Murray has received thousands of venomous letters. One contained a picture of her clipped from a newspaper and smeared with human excrement which still reeks when she shows it. Printed on it are these words: "This is my toast for you—here's crud in your eyes—and I hope somebody drops poison in your beer." Other pieces of mail, selected at random by me, and reported here only somewhat expurgated:

"Lady, you are as deadly to our city as a snake. Return to Russia. (signed) A True Believer in our God who gave you the air you breathe."

"You don't belong in this country. Russia is where you should go, and when you get there, kiss the hind end of dictator K. He is an atheist, too, and will be pleased to give you a big bear hug."

"You must be an insidious creature, without even a brain. No wonder you're crazy. You probably have no children either, let alone a man. Your hooked, ugly nose, triple chin, and fat 'slobby' body are enough to make you godless."

"You filthy atheist. Only a rat like you would go to court to stop prayer. All curses on you and your family. Bad luck and leprosy disease upon you and your damn family."

"You will repent, and damn soon a .30-30 (rifle bullet) will fix you nuts. You will have bad luck forever. You atheist, you mongrel, you good for nothing s——, you damn gutter rat. Jesus will fix you, you filthy scum."

What Do You Think?

1. Many states exempt private religious schools from property taxes. Some people feel that such states are actually supporting religious schools. Would you agree or not? Explain.
2. How do you explain the intolerance that has greeted Mrs. Murray?
3. Can hatred such as this be prevented? If so, how?

2.   THE EXTREMISTS ARE TAKING OVER *

*Hatred does much more than punish dissenting individuals. It can
also produce deep divisions within a society. The President's Commission on Civil Disorders warned that the United States is moving
toward a separate society of black and white. John Gardner, former
Secretary of Health, Education, and Welfare feels that the "moderates"
on both sides had better get involved, or the division will get worse.*

Most white people are neither haters nor practitioners of violence.
Nor are most Negroes. The majority of each race earnestly wishes that
constructive, non-violent solutions could be found to the racial problems
that rack—and may rack—the nation.

But there are whites that hate, and whites who advocate violence.
There are Negroes who do the same. And, unfortunately, the whites and
Negroes who do not hate and destroy too often quietly tolerate those who
do.

Those who hate and those who resort to violence—whether they are
white or black—cannot resolve the problems that divide this nation.
They can only intensify the senseless spasms of emotion and savage action.

There are many levels at which we must seek solutions to the problems which are tearing the nation apart. We must attack hard-core poverty with renewed vigor—through education, job-training, employment,
housing, and other measures. We must attack discrimination in every form.
We must take steps to ensure civil order.

But, at the same time that we are working on such basic problems,
we must cope with the upward spiral of mutual fear and corrosive hostility between white and Negro communities.

Hatred and violence used to be chiefly the stock-in-trade of the
white racist. Then they became the stock-in-trade of the Negro extremist.
Both justified their malevolence with cogent arguments.

But today there is a curious contrast between the two. Negro hatred
of whites is often expressed openly. It is frankly defended and widely
discussed. In contrast, white hatred of Negroes has gone underground.
It is rarely discussed publicly, rarely debated candidly. Indeed, when
the President's Commission on Civil Disorders spoke of it openly, many
people thought the authors of the report had done an unseemly thing.

Yet the white hatred is there. And everyone who reads this article
knows it. The long tradition of white brutality and mistreatment of the
Negro has diminished but has not come to an end.

---

* John W. Gardner in *The Reader's Digest,* June 1966.

It still excludes Negroes from white neighborhoods, and bars them from many job opportunities. No Negro reaches adulthood without having been through many experiences with whites that bruise his self-respect and diminish his confidence. That is hard for him to understand, living as he does in a society that bases its moral claims on the worth and dignity of the individual.

Such attitudes on the part of whites must come to an end if this nation is to survive as a free society. Each one who adds his bit to the storm of hatred does his share to move us toward a final reckoning that no free American will like.

Negro extremists who advocate violence assert that non-violence did not work. It is untrue. The greatest gains for the American Negro came in response to the non-violent campaigns of Martin Luther King, Jr., and (before it turned violent) the Student Non-violent Coordinating Committee.

It is the fashion now to belittle those gains, but they were great and undeniable. They were registered in historic civil-rights legislation and even more emphatically in social practice. Compare Negro voting patterns today with those prevailing as little as three years ago; or southern school desegregation today with practices of four years ago; or patterns of restaurant and hotel desegregation over the same period; or employment opportunities now and then.

The gains are not enough. They cannot satisfy our conscience. But they were substantial. And they came in response to non-violence.

The violent tactics of the past two years have brought nothing but deepened hostility between the two races and a slowing down of progress in the necessary drive toward social justice.

Many white liberals have now allied themselves with the Negro extremists in the sanctioning of violence. They speak approvingly of past riots as having "dramatized" the problem. They never speak of the negative consequences of the riots, but everyone who observed the session of Congress that followed the riots of 1967 knows that the negative reactions were a reality, and diminished the possibility of constructive solutions.

Nor do those who condone violence ever speak of the legacy of bitterness and division that will be left by increasingly harsh outbursts of destructive interaction. What good will it do to dramatize the problem if, in the process, hatreds burn themselves so deep that the wounds permanently cripple our society? Nor do those who condone violence ever face up to the likelihood that the paroxysms of public disorder will lead ultimately to authoritarian countermeasures.

One of the difficulties in halting the interplay of fear and violence is the tendency toward indiscriminate indictment of one race or the other. One man killed Martin Luther King—and Stokely Carmichael indicts the whole white race. A small minority of Negroes loot and burn, and many whites indict the whole Negro race.

Where will it lead? Negro extremists shout slogans of hate. White racists whisper their rage. Each justifies himself by pointing to acts of members of the other race. Hatred triggers violence, violence stirs further hatred, savage acts bring savage responses, hostility begets hostility, and the storm rages on. At some point, the terrifying interplay must have an end.

We must break through the terrible symmetry of action and reaction, assault and counterassault, hatred and responsive hatred. And the only way to do that is to ask the moderates on each side to cope with the haters and the doers of violence within their own ranks.

There is no way for the Negro moderate to curb the white extremist, or the white moderate to curb the Negro extremist. If they try, they just give further impetus to the interplay of hostility. That is why moderate whites must curb the haters within their own ranks, and moderate Negroes must curb their own extremists.

To date, the moderates—both Negro and white—have been all too silent. It was predictable. Moderates are alike, whatever their race. They don't want to become involved. They don't want to appear controversial. They don't like trouble.

But, increasingly, the extremists of both races are giving them trouble, whether they like it or not. And it will get worse before it gets better. It's time for the moderates to speak up and assert their strength.

This "revolt of the moderates" must go on day in and day out—in offices, factories, homes, and clubs. Those who promote hatred must be called to account. Those who commit or condone destructive acts must feel the full weight of disapproval by their friends and neighbors. Each contributes his little bit to the destruction of this society.

In a curious way, the whites who hate and destroy and the Negroes who hate and destroy are allies moving the rest of us toward a terrible climax. Martin Luther King understood that, and fought against both all his life, by word and deed. And so must all of us who care about the future of this society.

What Do You Think?

1. Why has "white hatred gone underground"?
2. Why do so many people, both black and white, prefer to stay on the sidelines?
3. What might be done to help prevent the division in our society that this author fears is emerging?

3. NO GOVERNMENT LOANS FOR STUDENT DISSENTERS *

The punishing of dissenters can take many forms. Here is another form that is used.

Senate and House conferees agreed yesterday on a compromise designed to stem the flow of federal loans and grants to students who engage in serious campus disturbances.

The curb on student rioters is part of a $7.2 billion three-year program of federal aid to colleges and universities.

Under the compromise, students would face loss of federal aid for a period of two years if:

Convicted by a court of any crime involving use of force, disruption of campus activities or seizure of college property.

He or she wilfully refused to obey lawful regulations or orders of college officials.

In both cases, funds could be ordered cut off only after opportunity for hearing and upon the finding that the offense was of a serious nature.

What Do You Think?

1. If you were a judge reviewing a case under this law, how would you decide upon:
   a. the constitutionality of the law?
   b. the difference between a "serious" offense and one "not serious"?
2. Should a student be given financial aid regardless of family income?
3. Are there some conditions which should be met before students can receive a government loan? Explain.

4. DISCRIMINATORY LAWS *

Rule by law is the basis of any democracy. But might laws be used to discriminate against and actually persecute dissenters? That is what this reading seems to suggest.

The war on dissent is by no means limited to opponents of the war in Vietnam. Even if that war does end soon, attempts to repress

---

* From *The New York Times,* October 1968.
* Excerpted from Nat Hentoff, "The War on Dissent," *Playboy,* September 1968. By permission of Nat Hentoff.

free speech and the right of assembly, among other legitimate democratic processes, will continue. Still vulnerable are the nation's black militants and some not so militant who just happen to be black. "Much of the troublemaking in the months and years ahead," Richard Rovere wrote in the same *New Yorker* article, "will be the work of Negroes, and I can even imagine the imposition of a kind of American apartheid—at least in the North, where Negroes live in ghettos that are easily sealed off."

Fanciful? Consider this memorandum about Chicago from Jay A. Miller of the American Civil Liberties Union there: "During the summer of 1967, we saw the machine attempt to use every possible and often lawless measure to 'keep a cool summer.' Using a mob-action statute, indiscriminate arrests and excessively high bail ($10,000–$50,000), they swept the streets of, and imprisoned without hearing, some 250–300 black citizens for a minimum of a week."

Several of those "lawless" measures were declared unconstitutional by a United States District Court judge in Chicago this past March. The city council, however, immediately enacted new ordinances that Jay Miller characterizes as being "worse than the old ones." Among them, for instance, is a stipulation that anyone continuing an activity deemed likely to lead to breach of the peace after the police have ordered him to stop can be charged with disorderly conduct. "Deemed likely" is so loose a term that it can encompass anyone the police want to seize. Similarly, there is another stipulation that anyone knowingly entering property open to the public and remaining there with "malicious or mischievous intent" give the police free reign to stop any demonstration they choose.

New York City, meanwhile, has passed emergency measures for "riots and other disorders" that are shocking in view of the fact that Mayor John V. Lindsay has long· been considered one of the country's most committed civil libertarians. The new measures, enacted last spring, severely restrict civil liberties by the imposition of curfews and the closing off of "disturbed" areas with accompanying harsh penalties for infractions of these emergency laws. The mayor is permitted to impose these restrictions on the free movement and free assembly of New Yorkers whenever he has "reason to believe that there exists a clear and present danger of a riot or other public disorder." As the New York Civil Liberties Union pointed out in a futile protest, "This condition does not pretend to be objective. It does not even require that a clear and present danger actually exist; it merely requires that the mayor believe it exists. He doesn't have to be right; he only has to be sincere. Such a provision truly substitutes the rule of men for the rule of law."

Just as startling is the power the mayor of New York now has to use his emergency measures if "an act of violence" has taken place. As the N. Y. C. L. U. also charged, "This condition is so vague as to be meaningless. Hardly a day passes without 'an act of violence.' The bill does not even bother to state whether or not the act of violence has to occur in New York City. It would appear that his bill permits the mayor to show the existence of a similar threat here. Had this bill been passed prior to the assassination of Martin Luther King, it would have permitted the mayor to restrict civil liberties in New York because of the possible effects of 'an act of violence' in Memphis."

And New York City is generally considered to be the most "liberal" in the country.

Philadelphia officials have also become expert in keeping their city "cool," whether or not a clear and present danger to the peace exists. A proclamation last summer prohibited "all persons . . . from gathering on the public streets or sidewalks in groups of 12 or more . . . except for recreational purposes in parks or other recreation areas." A similar proclamation was issued and enforced immediately after the murder of Martin Luther King. Precedents for immediate, arbitrary use of "emergency" powers are being set throughout the country, and they are dangerous precedents.

At the same time, individual dissenters are being repressed. In recent months, H. Rap Brown, national chairman of SNCC, has been undergoing a complicated series of court cases. When he was first released on bail, it was only on condition that he not leave the 11 counties of the southern district of New York, where the office of his lawyer, William Kunstler, is located. The judge who made the decision did not try to hide his intent: "Mr. Brown is not going to make speeches, because he is going to have to stay in Mr. Kunstler's district except when going to and from trial." For a time, the attempt to silence Brown worked. He had to cancel many speaking engagements in this country and abroad. When he finally did go to California to speak, he was jailed. And last May, he received the maximum sentence of five years in jail and a $2000 fine for violating the National Firearms Act. That law forbids anyone under a felony indictment to transport a gun across state lines. The charge against Brown was that while under a indictment for arson in Maryland, he carried a carbine in his luggage on a plane from New York to Baton Rouge last August. There is not only a serious question as to whether Brown did, indeed, know he was under indictment at the time but there is also the clear likelihood that he is being punished so severely in an attempt to silence him for as long as possible. At the time of Brown's sentencing in New Orleans on May 22, William Kunstler declared: "I would hate to think my country used a little-known law like this to persecute and silence this man." It did; and the case is now on appeal.

Another illustration of how dangerous it is becoming to be a militant black dissenter is what happened to Clifton Thirley Haywood, a Negro and a Muslim. Last October, he was given two consecutive five-year sentences and two $10,000 fines for violations of the Selective Service Act—the heaviest sentence for such violations of the Selective Service Act since World War One. The jail term and fines were imposed even though Haywood had told Judge Frank M. Scarlett of the United States District Court in Brunswick, Georgia, that he was willing to violate his religious beliefs and enter the Armed Forces. If Haywood were not black, and a Muslim besides, would the sentence have been that severe? Even Senator Richard Russell of Georgia knows the answer to that question.

In January of this year, poet-polemicist LeRoi Jones, charged with the possession of guns during the violence in Newark last summer, received nearly a maximum sentence—two and a half to three years, plus a $1000 fine, with no probation permitted. The reason: because of what LeRoi Jones has written—the First Amendment notwithstanding. The judge said explicitly that he made the sentence so severe in large part because of a poem by Jones that had appeared in the previous month's *Evergreen Review*. The poem, the judge, stated, was "antiwhite and full of obscenities." Only on the day of the sentencing was Jones or anyone else aware that he was also on trial for writing a poem. Reflecting on this ominous augury, Allen Ginsberg, gathering signatures for a writers' petition protesting the sentence, said: "I'm getting scared because of police-state purposes in this country. A lot of things I imagined in 'Howl' are, unfortunately, coming true. . . . LeRoi didn't have any pistols. I talked to his father and his wife and they both told me that LeRoi had told them in private that he didn't have any guns. I called California the other day to get people to sign the petition and found that Ferlinghetti and Baez were in jail. And now Spock. Everything has gotten serious in a very weird way."

In December, 1967, as news broke that Stokely Carmichael was coming home from his travels abroad, a number of congressmen prepared special greetings. While overseas, Carmichael had, indeed, spoken vehemently against American policies; but that was all he had done. He had given his opinions. Proclaimed Congressman Robert Michel of Illinois: "I rise to express my complete agreement with President Johnson on one point. I am referring to press reports that the President feels very strongly that Stokely Carmichael should be prosecuted for sedition if and when he returns to the United States."

This past spring, there were passionate speeches in Congress in opposition to the right of assembly in Washington of the members of the Poor People's Campaign that had been initiated by the late Martin Luther King. Bills were submitted to forbid the march, to deny the demonstrators access to the Capitol or its grounds and to campsites on public parkland. Senator Karl Mundt even accused Government officials of "lacking courage" to stand up against dissent.

What Do You Think?

1. The author suggests that there is a "war on dissent" in America today. Would you agree? Why or why not?

2. Do law enforcement agencies react differently to black dissent than to white? What about legislators?

5. THE POLICEMAN ORGANIZES *

Police (as well as teachers) are receiving better salaries but are showing signs of dissatisfaction with the role imposed upon them by society. As a result, many younger police officers, displaying a strong shift to the right among big city police, have organized themselves into LEG (Law Enforcement Group). As one veteran policeman indicated, "They're fighting back against what they consider an intolerable situation." Is the "situation" intolerable?

Robert Raggi, 29, is a patrolman in Brooklyn's 80th precinct. Raggi is also, and more to the point, a founding member of a newly established, militantly conservative organization of New York police officers called LEG (for Law Enforcement Group).

Indeed, patrolman Raggi has over the last few weeks come to symbolize a strong swing to the right among big-city police across the country—and young policemen in particular.

This accent on youth has worked to produce a far different picture of police-leftist frictions and clashes than is generally accepted. Instead of a confrontation between young radical demonstrators on the one side and wide-beamed, middle-aged cops on the other, the emerging picture portrays a collision of contemporaries.

DISPLEASED, TOO

There is nothing new in the fact that policemen everywhere tend to be conservative politically. But young officer Raggi and his colleagues in LEG bring something quite new to the stereotype of the cop as a steadfast defender of the establishment and a loyal guardian of the status quo.

In their own way these young officers of the right are as displeased with the current state of the republic as their opposite numbers in the new left.

---

* Reprinted from Richard Dougherty, "LEG and the Young Cops of the Right," *Los Angeles Times,* October 6, 1968. Copyright 1968, Los Angeles Times.

To Raggi and company the establishment is guilty of having saddled the country with public policies that are over-liberal, over-tolerant, over-permissive and therefore inimical to the police and the cause of effective law enforcement.

They are angry. Here is a veteran Manhattan police lieutenant commenting on LEG:

What we're seeing, I think, are dissident youth on the police force. They're exploding. They're fighting back against what they consider an intolerable situation. Just as there seems to be a new left on the campuses, there seems to be a new right among some younger men in the police department.

How significant is this youthful "explosion," not only in New York but in other American cities? That is hard to say. But it would seem highly significant when viewed in the light of the relative youth of most police forces, in the extent to which police everywhere applauded the Chicago department's handling of demonstrators at the Democratic convention, and in the popularity of George C. Wallace within the police community in general.

UNDER THIRTY

The powerful and traditionally conservative Patrolmen's Benevolent Association in New York has made no effort to play down the significance of patrolmen Raggi's LEG and—on the basis of departmental age statistics —it is easy to see why.

More than 10,000 New York officers, or something over a third of the country's largest force, are between the ages of 21 and 30.

Of these, 4500 are 25 or younger. The average age of patrolmen— the rank which provides the bulk of manpower assigned to demonstrations and pounding beats—is under 30. Almost half the entire department is under 35; and 80 per cent is 45 or younger.

The PBA, dominated by older men who have worked up through the association hierarchy, was clearly in no mood to extend a welcoming hand to LEG as, in a resolution passed recently, it declared that: "Radicalism and extremism in every form are to be shunned as contrary to the American democratic principles which are wholeheartedly supported by the vast majority of New York city patrolmen."

Nor have Mayor John V. Lindsay and police commissioner Howard R. Leary taken the emergence of LEG lightly, although they have refrained from expressing their displeasure in public. Privately, both admit to being disturbed by LEG and the possible effect it could have on police relations with the city's vast ghetto communities.

Leary—facing the promise of more trouble on Columbia University's campus, of rising tempers in the ghettos over the current school decentralization, of all the tensions the nation's biggest city is heir to—has his fingers crossed. According to one close friend, he "reminds himself every day that when you lose control of the cops, you've lost control of everything."

---

1. How do you explain the extremes among young people—the "New Left" on the campus, and the "New Right" on the police force?
2. Why do police feel it necessary to form such organizations as LEG?

6. DISSENT: POSITIVE FORCE OR IMMATURE PROTEST? *

One thing seems obvious: Reactions to dissent vary considerably. Here are some further views, both pro and con.

(Q) *Aren't students supposed to be learning—not demonstrating?*

YES! A university is a place where students come to learn. Among other things, they should learn to weigh important issues carefully, debate them coolly and fairly, and try to understand all viewpoints.

Protest demonstrations work against this end. As Columbia University's president, Grayson Kirk, has pointed out: "The . . . activities that constitute the life of this and every other university—teaching, discussions among faculty and students, scholarly and scientific investigation—cannot be carried on in an atmosphere of actual or threatened violence."

Nobody says that students shouldn't have strong opinions and make those opinions known. But there's a difference between expressing opinions and ramming them down other people's throats. Students who disrupt university life with their demands are saying, in effect, that they already know all the answers—"Don't teach us, we'll teach you."

George F. Kennan, former U. S. Ambassador to the Soviet Union, has said: "It is the student who is under obligation to the university and its sponsors, not vice versa. Higher education is not an absolute right, nor is the enjoyment of it devoid of responsibilities." Any college students who feel they have nothing more to learn should clear out and make room for others who do want to study.

NO! All through the 1950's students were continually criticized for

---

* From *World Week Magazine,* September 13, 1968. © 1968 by Scholastic Magazines, Inc.

being too apathetic. There were lots of problems in the world that needed solving—but Joe College and Betty Coed seemed to care more about fraternity parties and the number of people they could fit into a phone booth.

Now things have changed. Students are demonstrating because they are learning things and are acting on their knowledge. Demonstrations are only one result of this trend—the one that gets most publicity. Many students are also tutoring underprivileged children, working in ghettos, and helping out in election campaigns. All this, too, is "student power"— and it ought to be earning students a good name.

As U. S. Supreme Court Justice Abe Fortas has said, the current youth revolt "may pressage a new and welcome era of idealism in the nation. . . . It presents a challenge to the older generation as well as to youth to reconsider the goals of society and its values."

In today's world, people can't always wait until their knowledge is complete before they form opinions. It's unreasonable to expect all students to shut themselves up in an ivory tower and stay "uninvolved" during their college years. If we want our students to become responsible, involved citizens, we should expect them to start getting involved now.

(Q) *Aren't student protestors only a noisy minority?*

YES! The protests at Columbia University were begun by about 300 students out of a total enrollment of more than 17,500. Even when the demonstrations were at their peak, only about 1,500 people took part. At Columbia and other universities, groups of equal size have actively opposed the demonstrators and their tactics.

A recent Gallup Poll revealed that only one out of five college students on the nation's campuses has ever taken part in a demonstration. In too many cases a minority is trying to force its views on the majority of students whose primary interest is in getting an education. And as Robben W. Fleming, president of the University of Michigan, has said: "A great university is a place where neither the tyranny of the majority nor the minority is acceptable."

Even more important, the small groups which usually spark protests are often led by radicals who are out for their own political purposes, not the students'. They're not really interested in specific issues, they just want the opportunity to disrupt "The Establishment" as a step toward overthrowing all authority.

As Mark Rudd, an organizer of the demonstrations at Columbia, wrote to the university president: "If we win, we will take control of your world, your corporation, your university. . . ." These are not the words of someone who wants to improve either the university or society.

NO! People who feel that student protesters can be dismissed as a noisy but unimportant minority are only kidding themselves. There is widespread agreement among many of today's undergradutes that many things in society are going badly and need to be changed. Students are particularly concerned about the Viet Nam war, the draft, and racial problems. Such concern has spearheaded many of the protests.

Most of the protests that have broken out at universities cannot be explained away merely as the work of "extremists" who spend all their time organizing conspiracies. For they have also been backed by large numbers of not-so-extreme students who are uneasy enough about things to be willing to go out and join the protest.

The "radical fringe" is like the mere tip of an iceberg that appears above the surface of the ocean. Beneath this tip is a much larger mass of students who tend to feel the same way, but are perhaps less energetic or less vocal in expressing their ideas.

The actual number of persons arrested at Columbia was small compared to the total university enrollment, but they represented students willing to face arrest and risk their future careers for what they believe in. After all, many important events in history—for example, the American Revolution—have been caused by "small minorities."

(Q) *Aren't most student demands vague and irresponsible?*

YES! Many students lack the patience to work within democratic means to achieve what they want. It is much simpler to draw up a list of demands and threaten to disrupt the university unless these demands are met. Sometimes the demands are even for things beyond the power of any university to grant. And often these demands, such as the right to use "filthy speech," are silly.

Harvard University president Nathan M. Pusey has attributed some campus disorders to the "belligerent nonsense" of students "safe within the sanctuary of an ordered society, dreaming of glory, . . . playing at being revolutionaries, and fancying themselves rising to positions of command atop the debris as the structures of society come crashing down."

Too often the protesting students are interested only in acts of defiance toward their elders. Some student leaders have even boasted that if 10 demands are met by college authorities, they will present 10 new ones. And some student demonstrations have even occurred after policy reforms have been made.

NO! In any movement there are bound to be people who are participating for the wrong reasons. Students who demand the right to use "filthy speech" are either immature or just having fun at the expense of other students who care about the issues they are demonstrating about.

The decision to resort to a massive protest often just "happens" because of the frustration of many students who have sought changes through more conventional means. Let's face it: Some university administrations are anything but democratic. Decisions which affect the well-being and future lives of students are often made by a small group of trustees and senior faculty members who do not fully consider how times have changed since they were in school.

Most students do not make demands and organize demonstrations just because they enjoy defying their elders. They do it because it is often the only means left open to them by parents, administrators, or public officials who repeatedly ignore young people's legitimate needs and wishes.

What Do You Think?

1. One argument against dissent presented in this reading is that students should be "learning" rather than "doing"? How would you respond to this? Explain.
2. Is there a danger in America today of "tyranny by the minority"? How can this be guarded against?
3. Why are there so few student protests against the protestors?
4. How would you respond to the questions asked in this reading?

7. A PLEA FOR RESTRAINT *

Thoreau went to jail for refusing to pay his taxes during the Mexican war, but he did not lie down in front of the wagons bound for that war. Does the civil disobedience of today's dissenters go too far?

We live in a society . . . where government and order are not only a necessity but are the preference of an overwhelming majority of the citizenry. . . . Inevitably there are occasions when individuals or groups will chafe under a particular legal bond or will bridle in opposition to a particular governmental policy; and the question presents itself: What can be done?

Vocal objection, of course—even slanderous or inane—is permissible. But the fact that one is a dissenter with a right to express his opposition entitles him to no special license. . . .

The right to disagree . . . does not authorize [individuals] to carry on their campaign of education and persuasion at the expense of someone

---

* Excerpted from Erwin Griswold, "The Right to Differ Has Limits," *The Christian Science Monitor,* July 20, 1968. Reprinted from "Dissent—1968," by Erwin N. Griswold, June 1968, *Tulane Law Review,* Vol. 42–4.

else's liberty. . . . Violent opposition to law . . . proceeds on the foolhardy . . . principle that might makes right. . . .

LEGAL OR MORAL RIGHTS

You will note that I imply that a line may be drawn between legal and moral rights to dissent . . . that there may be a moral right to dissent without a corresponding legal privilege to do so. It is in this context that "civil disobedience" must be viewed. . . .

I mean by "civil disobedience" the deliberate violation of a rule ordained by constituted government because of a conscientious conviction that the law is so unjust that it cannot morally be observed by the individual. . . .

This decision . . . should be made only after the most painful and introspective reflection and only when the firm conclusion is reached that obedience offends the most fundamental personal values. . . .

Henry David Thoreau is generally regarded as the most notable American exponent of civil disobedience, and all of us share admiration for his determination. But we must not ignore the vital aspect of Thoreau's nonconformity: his passionate attempt to dissociate himself from society. . . .

A DIFFERENT CENTURY

Thoreau's poignant attitude was charming enough in mid-19th-century America. But it was essentially an effort to withdraw from the realities of life and it was . . . myopic [1] even then; for it was painfully inconsistent with the fact that man is a part of society by nature, by geography, and by citizenship. . . . There is nothing noble or salutary about foredoomed attempts to abdicate membership in society. . . .

This is precisely what nonconformity as a way of life is. It is the essential irrationality of the "hippie movement"—a mass endeavor to drop out of life. . . .

Stretched to its logical extreme, this also is civil disobedience, and for this reason I urge that before any man embarks upon a unilateral nullification of any law, he must appreciate that his judgment has not merely a personal significance but also portends grave consequences for his fellows.

GANDHIAN TRADITION

In determining whether and when to exercise the moral right to disobey the dictates of the law, it must also be recognized that society . . . cannot recognize this determination as entitled to legal privilege.

---

[1] nearsighted

It is part of the Gandhian tradition of civil disobedience that the sincerity of the individual's conscience presupposses that the law will punish this assertion of personal principle. . . . For this reason one who contemplates civil disobedience out of moral conviction should not be surprised . . . if a criminal conviction ensues. . . . His hope is that he may aid in getting the law changed. But if he does not succeed in that, he cannot complain if the law is applied to him. . . .

A proper recognition of the rights of conscience is one of the basic assumptions of our society. The problem, of course, is to determine what is "proper." . . .

DRAMATIC EXAMPLES

Lunch-counter sit-ins and freedom rides are among the most dramatic examples of the techniques that were used to expose the injustices that were perpetrated under the banner of law. In many of these cases, these actions were not, indeed, illegal, since the restrictive laws were plainly invalid. . . . In other cases, though, the line was not clear, and sometimes the actions taken were undoubtedly illegal.

We cannot fail to recognize the fact that it was these tactics which succeeded in putting the basic issues squarely before the courts and the public. And it was in this way that the law was clarified in the courts and that legislative changes were brought about. . . .

In retrospect, I am sure that our nation will point with pride not only to the courage of those who risked punishment in order to challenge injustice, but also to the morality of their actions in scrupulously avoiding violence, even in reaction to the force which was exerted on them. The affirmation of the close relation between morality and nonviolence will be one of the many monuments of the Rev. Dr. Martin Luther King, Jr.

As this experience shows, the ultimate legal success as well as the intrinsic moral quality of civil disobedience turns on the restraint with which it is exercised.

What Do You Think?

1. How should a society decide whether or not a law is unjust? How would you decide?
2. Would you agree with the author that the hippie movement is in the category of civil disobedience? Why or why not?
3. Can you think of any laws that you would consider "illegal," or immoral? Explain.

8. IS LONG HAIR UNCONSTITUTIONAL? *

In November of 1968 the United States Supreme Court refused to hear a case involving a dispute with school authorities over long hair. The reason for the refusal was that at least six Justices felt that no federal issue was involved. (Four Justices must approve, or a case will not be accepted.) One of the dissenters was Justice Douglas, who did feel that the case came rightfully under the Federal Constitution. If you were a Supreme Court Justice, how would you have voted? What would your reasons be?

The setting is a small town in a midwestern state where a young man has been suspended from the local high school for appearing with a "Prince Charles" haircut. The boy's family has decided to appeal the principal's decision, and has sought legal aid from the American Civil Liberties Union. The ACLU responded to the request by providing an attorney.

A meeting of the Board of Trustees of the school district is called, and, as the scene opens, the attorney for the ACLU is questioning the counsel representing the Board. There is an audience of about 200 persons.

(Q) How much authority does a school have in the matter of control over children?

(A) I will read you the pertinent section of the State law. It says "the school has the right to exercise the same authority as to conduct and behavior over the pupils attending school . . . during the time they are in attendance . . . as the parents may exercise over them."

(Q) Do you think hair style can be called "conduct" or "behavior"?
(A) Yes, I do.

(Q) I don't see how you can come to that conclusion. But even if hair style is "behavior," isn't the school prescribing a child's behavior at home, since he cannot take his hair off at school and paste it back on at home?

(A) You are confusing the issue. We are only concerned here with the regulations that apply to a child while he is in school. Freakish styles of hairdo distract the attention of other students, and therefore disrupt the orderly procedure of learning.

(Q) But can't the teacher crack down on any students who "disrupt"?

---

* Adapted from Spencer Coxe, "The Great Hair Problem," reprinted by permission of *Youth* Magazine, published by the United Church Press for teenagers of the United Church of Christ, the Episcopal Church, Church of the Brethren, and the Anglican Church of Canada.

(A) Teachers already have enough difficulty with the rebellious youth of today. Why do you want to add to their troubles?

(Q) I don't, and I believe that if the teacher ignored the hair there would be little or no disruption. (Applause from scattered sections of the room) At this point, I would like to raise the issue of constitutionality. Will you not agree that it is the intention of the First Amendment to guarantee freedom of expression? And would it not follow that a hairdo is a form of self-expression?

(A) That's stretching the First Amendment pretty far. Long hair protected by the First Amendment! Who ever heard of such a crazy idea? I guess mini-skirts and granny dresses are protected too. (Laughter and scattered applause)

(Q) Why not? Why must we limit freedom of expression to speech or writing? Why can't we admit that there are some people who, for one reason or another, need to express their individuality in some other way?

(A) In all your arguments you are forgetting the central fact that it is the function of the school to teach young people respect for authority. If youngsters can do anything they please, the school ceases to operate as a place of learning. As an attorney, you should know the importance of law and order.

(Q) I do . . . but as an attorney, I say that rules should be reasonable, that there should be a compelling necessity for any rule—not just some pet idea of the principal or School Board. Can't you see this?

(A) But this happens to be a case of "compelling necessity," as you call it.

(Q) Compelling in what sense? Is the health or safety of the other children involved? I would agree with a principal's rule that girls do not wear highly inflammable clothing in cooking class, or that boys on the school football team must wear protective gear. But what is the "compelling necessity" in this case?

(A) Schools must have rules that make the educational process an orderly one. It seems to me that the organization you represent wants to promote anarchy rather than a sound school system. In any case, I suppose "obedience" is a dirty word in your vocabulary, but it's not in mine.

(Q) That is not so. Your kind of obedience is blind obedience, the kind that cannot be justified by reasonable argument. May I remind you that this nation was created by "disobedient" men who saw no sense to the rules imposed on them?

(A) May I remind you that "comparisons are odious"? Those men were probably very obedient in school.

(Q) Well, I can see that there is no point in going on any further, but I would like to raise one final question, and that is this: it is one of the characteristics of the police state, such as the former Nazi Germany or Communist China today, that everyone dresses alike, because it is quite obvious that everyone dressing alike promotes thinking and acting alike. Members of the Board, ladies and gentlemen, is this what we want in this country?

(At the end of the meeting, the school board votes in favor of the ruling of the principal.)

What Do You Think?

1. Does the First Amendment intend to limit "speech" only to the spoken word, or does it include other forms of expression?
2. Should students be allowed to participate in making laws that regulate student behavior?
3. What guidelines would you set for drawing up "reasonable" school regulations?

9. HAVE THE DISSENTERS GONE TOO FAR? *

Not all reactions to dissent involve force or violence. Some are verbal and raise some provocative points. Eric Sevareid, the news commentator, supports the right to dissent, but questions the content and manner of much of today's dissent.

When we reach the point, which we have, where an organization is formed, called "Proxy Pickets," to rent out picketers for any cause at so much an hour, then we know that the fine, careless rapture of this era of protest is all over and that the corruption of faddism has begun to set in. Every movement becomes an organization sooner or later, then a kind of business, often a racket. This is becoming the age of the Cause. Kids will soon be hanging around back lots trading causes the way they used to trade aggies.

One of the oddest things about the period, no doubt, is that anyone like me should feel moved to say these things. I have always believed in the Negro "revolution," if that's the right word. I have not believed, for some time now, in the Vietnamese war because to me the official

* Reprinted from Eric Sevareid, "Dissent or Destruction," *Look,* September 5, 1967. Copyright 1967 by Eric Sevareid. Reprinted by permission of Harold Matson Company, Inc.

rationale for it simply does not add up, and as a college kid in the thirties, I was a hollering "activist" and even voted for the Oxford oath— "I will not fight for flag or country" (though I couldn't sleep that night for doubts about it, which will merely prove to today's hip set that I had the seeds of squaredom in me at an early age).

But it seems clear to me now that a high percentage of today's protests, in these three areas of civil rights, the Vietnam war and college life —all of which commingle at various points—have gone so far as to be senselessly harming the causes themselves, corroding the reputations of the most active leaders and loosening some of the cement that holds this American society together. There never was any real danger that this country would find itself groaning under Fascist oppression, but there is a measure of real danger that freedom can turn into nationwide license until the national spirit is truly darkened and freedom endangered.

The notion is abroad that if dissent is good, as it is, then the more dissent the better, a most dubious proposition. The notion has taken hold of many that the manner and content of their dissent are sacred, whereas it is only the right of dissent that is sacred. Reactions of many dissenters reveal a touch of paranoia. When strong exception is taken to what they say by the President or by a General Westmoreland, the dissenters cry out immediately that free speech is about to be suppressed, and a reign of enforced silence is beginning.

What is more disturbing is that a considerable number of liberal Left activists, including educated ones, are exhibiting exactly the spirit of the right-wing McCarthyites 15 years ago, which the liberal Left fought so passionately against in the name of our liberties. For the life of me, I cannot see the difference in morality between the right-wing woman in Texas who struck Ambassador Adlai Stevenson and the left-wing students and off-campus characters at Dartmouth College who howled down ex-Governor Wallace of Alabama and tried to smash his car.

The use of force to express a conviction, even if it takes so relatively mild a form as a college sit-in that blocks an administration building, is intolerable. When [a man like] Dr. Martin Luther King, who may well . . . [have been] one of the noblest Americans of the century, deliberately defies a court order, then he ought to go to jail. Laws and ordinances can be changed, and are constantly being changed, but they cannot be rewritten in the streets where other citizens also have their rights.

I must say that, kooky as we may have been in that first real American student movement in the thirties, we never, to my memory, even dreamed of using force. We thought of the university, much as we often hated its official guts, as the one sanctuary where persuasion by reason must rule alone and supreme, if the university itself were to be preserved from the outside hands of force and unreason. What makes today's college activists think they can take the campus forcibly into national politics without national politics—in the form of police or legislature or troops—forcibly coming onto the campus? (Some of the activists, of course, are pure nihilists and want this to happen, but that's another story.)

The wild riots that have exploded in the Negro areas of American cities the last few summers should not be confused with protest movements. Most of them do not even deserve the designation of race riot. We had genuine race riots in Chicago, Detroit, and Tulsa nearly half a century ago, whites against Negroes, and mass murders occurred. Nearly all the recent summer-night riots have chiefly involved Negro kids smashing and looting the nearest property, most of which was owned by other Negroes. This is sheer hoodlumism, involved as its psychological and sociological origins may be. It is a problem for sociologists, psychologists, and economists only in the second instance. In the first instance, it is a police problem, as are the episodes of mass vandalism staged by prosperous white kids on the beaches of New Hampshire or Florida. Majorities have a right to protection quite as much as minorities, heretical as this may sound.

What Do You Think?

1. Are many dissenters paranoid in their attitudes, as Mr. Sevareid suggests?

2. Has the protest movement become a fad (like long hair or love beads)?

3. Would you agree that there is no danger of "Fascist oppression" taking over in this country? Why or why not?

4. Do law enforcement officials have the right to control the *manner* and *content* of dissent? Explain.

ACTIVITIES FOR INVOLVEMENT

1. Barry Goldwater, the Republican candidate for President in 1964, said, in accepting the nomination, that "extremism in the defense of liberty is no vice." Write your interpretation of what Mr. Goldwater meant, and then compare your essay with those of your classmates. Be prepared to explain whether you agree or disagree with Mr. Goldwater, and why.

2. Have a mock trial of a university student accused of using violence in a dispute with the university administration.

3. Prepare a debate on the topic: Resolved: That civil disobedience is a justifiable means for expressing dissent.

4. By way of summary, arrange a class discussion that will set in focus the total picture of dissent—of youth, minorities and individuals—keeping in mind the following points:

   a. What is the motive for the dissent?

    b. What methods have been used to express the dissent?

    c. How have others reacted to this dissent?

    d. If there is dissent among the dissenters, why is this?

    e. What might be the long-range effect of the dissent?

    5.   To what extent has violence been a part of American life? H. Rap Brown once said that "violence is as American as apple pie." A group of students can explore the background of this question by consulting the Reader's Guide to Periodical Literature for articles on the topic. Give a panel report to the class by assigning each member a specific area, such as "war," "resistance to war," "riots," "lynching," etc.

    6.   Divide the class into three groups representing the far left, the moderates, and the far right. Have each group draw up a summary of its stand on dissent, civil disobedience, and violence. Select one person from each group to present the summary to the class for discussion.

    7.   Teachers have been fired from their jobs for speaking or writing against official policy. Invite a member of one of the teacher organizations in your district to discuss some of these cases. Organizations could include the American Federation of Teachers, the National Education Association, or other local groups.

    8.   The word "backlash" is often used to indicate the reaction against riots, civil-rights demonstrations, and civil disobedience. For class discussion, consider the topic: Will increased dissent bring about a backlash in the form of stricter laws and controls?

    9.   As is evident in the preceding readings, people react to dissent in various ways. In trying to assess the reasons for different reactions, discuss the importance or nonimportance of the following factors:

    a. The tendency to conformity.

    b. The fear of new ideas.

    c. Prejudice.

    d. Patriotism.

    e. Bigotry (religious prejudice).

    f. Greed.

    g. Power (the reluctance to give up a position of authority).

Rank these from 1 (most important) to 7 (least important) and then compare your rankings with those of your classmates. How would you explain any discrepancies that occur?

What Should Be Done About Dissent?

Most people would agree that the right of dissent is protected by the First Amendment to the Constitution, but there is wide disagreement as to how far that right extends. Even the Justices of the Supreme Court of the United States cannot agree. Are the freedoms in the Bill of Rights absolute freedoms? Or are some limits essential? If there are limits, where do we draw the lines between the goal of maximum personal freedom and the rights and safety of others? Should dissent be encouraged? Restricted?

1. JAIL THE DISSENTER? *

Should dissenters be jailed? For what kinds of dissent? The author suggests that the police make arrests for certain kinds of illegal behavior, but ignore others. Is a jail sentence too severe a punishment?

Nobody is opposed to civil disobedience; people simply want the laws that they deem important to be vigorously enforced and those they consider unfair to be ignored. Most motorists consider the idea of a speed trap outrageous, but rarely complain when policemen conceal themselves in public washrooms to ferret out homosexuals. The annual antics of American Legion conventioneers are viewed as harmless enough fun, but let political protestors go out in the streets and all the rigors of the law relating to trespass, obstruction of traffic, and disturbing the

---

* Excerpted from Joseph L. Sax, "Civil Disobedience: The Law Is Never Blind," *Saturday Review*, September 28, 1968. Copyright Saturday Review, Inc., 1968.

peace are suddenly remembered, whereupon we are solemnly told that acquiescence in illegality is the first step on the road to anarchy.

Through the miracle of prosecutorial discretion—a device central to the operation of the legal system, but widely ignored in discussions of civil disobedience—criminality can be, and is, produced or ignored virtually at will by law enforcement officials. Businessmen know that if the building and fire laws were fully implemented they could be in court virtually every day, a fact which is allegedly brought home to them when they are so unwise as to refrain from buying tickets to the annual policemen's ball.

Justice Jackson once said that "a prosecutor has more control over life, liberty, and reputation than any other person in America . . . he can choose his defendant . . . a prosecutor stands a fair chance of finding at least a technical violation of some act on the part of almost anyone." No more profound statement was ever made about the legal system.

The law is so vast in its technical coverage and so open-ended in its possibilities for interpretation by police officers, prosecutors, and judges that it becomes almost meaningless to talk about civil disobedience as if there were conduct which "the law"—as some external force—declared illegal.

In fact, no society could operate if it did not tolerate a great deal of technically or arguably illegal conduct on the ground that certain laws were obsolescent and others unwise as written or as applied to particular situations. A few weeks ago, newspapers carried the story of a man who had lured several boys to a mountain cabin, bound and then sexually abused them. One of the boys worked himself free, seized a rifle, and killed his abductor. The local prosecutor announced that no proceedings against the boy were contemplated, a result undoubtedly approved by every reader. Because the law of self-defense is so restrictive in permitting the use of deadly force, a technical case of murder might have been made out against the boy; the circumstances, however, made clear that it would have been unjust to prosecute. It is not strict obedience to the law, but the sense of justice, which we require in the administration of the legal system.

The same breadth of discretion which produced justice in the case of the abducted boy can be turned toward less attractive ends, depending on the inclinations of those who are charged with administering the law. To be sure, such discretion is not generally exercised arbitrarily. It is used to "fill the interstices," as lawyers sometimes put it—that is, to act in accordance with what it is thought the legislature would have done if it had considered the particular circumstances of the pending case. It is only a special class of cases which ordinarily raise the danger of unjust manipulation—those where political considerations make prosecution indiscreet or, conversely, where there are special political incentives to go forward.

In the former category are cases where the rich and the powerful find themselves able to "settle" potential criminal prosecutions. Thus, the Southern oligarchs were not indicted for criminal conspiracy when they produced their massive resistance campaign against the school integration decision, or led the fight to stand in the schoolhouse door, while Dr. Spock and other war resisters were readily brought to trial under the umbrella of the vague and amorphous conspiracy doctrine.

No one who sat through the four weeks of trial in which Benjamin Spock, William Sloane Coffin, Mitchell Goodman, and Michael Ferber were convicted of conspiracy to abet violation of the draft law could have doubted that Judge Francis Ford was persuaded of the rightness of the Government's case against them, or that the trial reflected his persuasion. The fact that one of the five defendants was ultimately acquitted is not a tribute to the fairness of the trial, but is, rather, a measure of the sloppiness with which the Government put its case together.

The first question is what social good is to be achieved by incarcerating men like Spock, Coffin, Goodman, and Ferber. They do not present the immediate danger to others of those who commit violent acts. Indeed, by advocating a form of passive resistance to governmental fiat, they operate at one of the least abrasive levels of conduct respecting an impact on the rights or property of others.

Moreover, the nature of their resistance is such that a layer of governmental decision is always imposed between their action and the prospect of harm to others. For example, it is clearly less intrusive for one opposed to school integration to boycott the schools than it is to stand in the doorway and prevent others from entering. And the boycott is very far removed from the acts of those who express their dissent by throwing a stone or a bomb. This is not to suggest that passive resistance should always be insulated from legal sanctions, but merely that the society's willingness to tolerate such conduct should be much greater than for direct action.

Another conventional rationale for incarceration is the desire to deter others similarly inclined. Where dissenting political activity is involved, history strongly suggests the inefficacy of such a response. One is hard-pressed to cite a political movement which has been suppressed through the jailing of its leaders. While it was said in the Spock-Coffin case that the prosecution was not directed at ideology, but rather at particular conduct, the record suggests the dubiousness of the distinction made by the Government between thought and action.

The defendants were charged only with talking and publishing, collecting and returning some draft cards, and engaging in peaceful demonstrations. Even the Government did not urge that any of this conduct in itself put a significant burden on the prosecution of its policies. The essence of the Government's case was that the defendants' persuasiveness and prestige were an incitement to young men to resist the draft—not that their touching of draft cards, or any such formal acts, were at the heart of the danger which they supposedly posed to the state. Yet it was the formal act of participating in a draft card return which made the Government's technical legal case against them. Upon such sands is the difference between criminality and innocence built in "the law." A common-sense inquiry into the justice of their prosecution makes it easy to see that it was their respectability, ideology, and force-fulness which were really at stake. Those elements are not likely to be amenable to incarceration.

As one turns away from legalistic thinking about the problems of protest, it becomes apparent that no large, general formulae are going to resolve the infinitely varied issues which arise. In the common situation where a group of housewives block a bulldozer's path to protest the destruction of a park, for example, there are at least two good reasons to refrain from prosecution at the outset, though technically a conviction might easily be obtained for trespassing or the obstruction of traffic. Often such a maneuver is designed to inform the general public of an unknown situation and to promote more serious consideration by the appropriate public officials.

Certainly these are acceptable goals, and as a practical matter only newspaper publicity is likely to be an effective prod. Considering the tendency of the papers to ignore less dramatic moves and the generally minimal adverse impact on the project by a few days' obstruction, the ladies' tactic would seem an appropriate and tolerable means of promoting the political process. We ought not to balk at taking into account the reality that a neighborhood group is unlikely to be very effective in going through the more conventional channels used by established lobbies or that they are unlikely to have the means to produce a substantial paid advertising campaign.

What Do You Think?

1. What constitutional issue is involved when a person is sentenced for "advocating" something?
2. Do the rich have special privileges before the law?
3. Do jail sentences deter others from engaging in dissent?

2. USE A FIRM HAND? *

In following selection the writer suggests that the best way to deal with dissent is to use "a firm hand." Can dissent be restrained in this way?

No society has ever tolerated unbridled license disguised as free speech, if only because society would come apart at the seams if it did any such thing. There are all kinds of restrictions on our right to sound off. There always have been.

For instance, I can't urge someone to dismember you with a carving knife. You can't accuse me of wife-beating, either—unless, of course, you can prove it. And Justice Holmes' acid comment upon the "right" of some joker to yell "Fire!" in a crowded theater is too well-known to warrant repeating here. No one can use the Constitution to advance the cause of riot, obscenity, or treason.

Our college students ought to be old enough to understand this. They ought to be able to understand something else, too: that the purpose of an institution of higher learning is not to afford them a built-in public address system and a captive audience.

It is to make them learned. It is to teach them to pursue the truth and to recognize it when and if they catch up with it. It is to hand from one generation to the next the intellectual artifacts which are the rungs of the great ladder leading us over the centuries from savagery to civilization.

Students are in school to learn, not to instruct—to listen, not to shoot their mouths off. When they have become at least partially educated, they may be worth listening to by the rest of us. Until that time, quite frankly, they are not. If they were already well-grounded in the cultural heritage of the race and in the ability to think in an orderly and disciplined fashion, there would be no need for them to be in college at all.

A court of justice doesn't permit unlimited free speech within its halls. Try it and see how quickly you land in contempt of court. Congress doesn't allow spectators in the gallery to harangue it under cover of the Third Amendment. No church in its right ecclesiastical mind will let some nut in the congregation stand up in the middle of Sunday services and bellow random blasphemies.

Why should a college or university be any different?

In public institutions, we address our peers in accordance with rules

---

* Excerpted from Max Rafferty, "Principal Ingredient for Settling Campus Uproars: A Firm Hand," *Los Angeles Times,* February 7, 1966.

previously set us through democratic processes. We do not unilaterally insist upon imposing our own whims and crotchets upon others and then shouting "Free speech!" when some of those others object to having to listen to us.

The Berkeley demonstrations and the illegitimate progeny which they have spawned across the land all stem from the refusal of the demonstrators to recognize one abiding truth: that in a democratic society, the small minority does not try to impose its will upon the great majority by force.

In a totalitarian state, such goings-on are par for the course.

Who knows? Maybe this is what the "new activists" are trying to get us conditioned to.

What Do You Think?

1. Is the right of free speech an absolute right? Why or why not?
2. Should university students only be concerned with the process of "learning," and not become involved in issues outside this sphere?
3. Should Communists who are American citizens be allowed to speak on campus?

3.   IS CONTINUAL INVESTIGATION NECESSARY? *

For many years the House Un-American Activities Committee has held investigations of individuals and groups suspected of being involved in a Communist conspiracy to subvert the government of the United States. The HUAC and its supporters feel that it is necessary to ferret out real or potential threats to the American way of life. But in the following selection, compiled by the American Civil Liberties Union, the central question is this: Are the methods employed by the Committee consistent with the democratic process or are they more closely related to the methods employed in totalitarian states? Would you support the actions of the HUAC as one solution to the question of dissent in the United States?

Many clergymen view as a moral imperative the lending of their prestige to the search for a peaceful world and the avoidance of nuclear warfare. They have been joined in this quest by many citizens who have never before been politically active. These people possess such a deep

---

* Excerpted from "The Case Against the House Un-American Activities Committee," pamphlet issued by the American Civil Liberties Union, New York.

concern with problems of peace and disarmament that many are joining various organizations for the first time in their adult lives. For them a HUAC investigation, accompanied by the usual publicity, is an especially frightening experience.

This was the case when the Committee undertook in 1962 an investigation of the extent of Communist infiltration into American peace groups. One of the groups singled out for attention was the Women's Strike for Peace, a volunteer group of women who had banded together to express concern with ways of avoiding nuclear war and attaining worldwide disarmament and peace. The group consisted of mothers and housewives, teachers, writers, social workers and other professional women.

Two-day hearings held in Washington, D. C., in December, 1962, evoked country-wide opposition to the Committee's tarring with a broad "Red" brush the loosely-organized WSP and other groups working for increased public discussion and action on peace issues. The barrage of criticism leveled at the Committee can be understood in light of the HUAC's statement, issued prior to the hearings, explaining the purpose of the investigation: *"Excessive concern with peace* (italics ours) on the part of any nation impedes or prevents adequate defense preparation, hinders effective diplomacy in the national interest, undermines the will to resist, and saps national strength. For these reasons, in today's world, intense peace propaganda and agitation in non-Commuist nations obviously serves the aggressive plans of world Communism."

Although the Committee added that it believes many persons sincerely seeking peace are not Communists since the desire for peace is "universal," it maintained that the utmost vigilance is still necessary in the conduct of peace activities to prevent Communist infiltration. The kind of vigilance exercised by the HUAC's own "exposure" practices will, as the ACLU said at the time, "stifle the voices of those who dissent from government policies in the Cold War. The immediate effect of the investigation will be to deter private citizens from participating in groups and activities which are concerned with a deeply felt need, and thus impose a mantle of conformity over a segment of our society. . . ."

Other voices raised against the Committee's philosophy and tactics during this hearing included that of famous cartoonist Herblock, who showed a late-arriving Committee member asking a colleague: "What are we against—Women or Peace?" Also airing criticism were editorial columnist Russell Baker of the *New York Times,* and syndicated columnists Inez Robb and Sydney J. Harris who spoke out sharply against the HUAC efforts to link peace groups with Communism.

"It is monstrous," wrote Miss Robb, "to permit peace and its advocacy to become criminal matters merely because the Russians have cynically used peace for propaganda." Columnist Harris defended WSP members as "women who are taking their responsibilities of citizenship seriously;

unlike the bulk of us who awaken out of our torpor once every few years to vote and then subside into self-centeredness."

At least six known cases of mistaken identity in the 1950's provide further graphic evidence of how badly Committee files are handled.

One of the most dramatic—and tragic—was that of a Hollywood screenwriter whose work, after a promising beginning, was suddenly unsalable anywhere in Hollywood. After five years, as he was beginning to believe he had lost his talent, he discovered his name was almost identical with that of a California clothier who had been "cited" by the Committee. The writer "cleared" himself, finally, in the movie industry, by carrying around a letter from the HUAC indicating that he was not the same person listed in the files. As New York Times reporter Murray Schumach wrote in an interview with the screenwriter: "(He) took back the letter and folded it carefully in his portfolio. He shook his head. 'Now I feel numb,' he said. 'But I can't help thinking that in those five long years nobody ever asked me once: Are you this man? Could you be this man? Nobody ever asked me.' "

But even the HUAC "clearance" made no difference to fearful movie executives. The New York Times, in reporting the screenwriter's death in 1964, said: "Despite the clearance, (he) found Hollywood doors still closed to him, and during recent years he turned to TV scripts under an assumed name—the only way, he said, that he could sell his work."

In another case, Mrs. Agnes Meyer, an outspoken Committee critic and influential Washington, D. C., educator, was accused by the HUAC of writing a pro-Russian article for a Russian newspaper. Close investigation showed the article was written by a Canadian woman with a closely similar name. It took the threat of a libel suit to make the Committee admit its error. However, Congressman Harold Velde, the HUAC chairman, justified the incident by saying "it was better to wrongly accuse one person of being a Communist than to allow many to get away with Communist acts . . ."

A schoolteacher in Mexico City found her name listed in a newsmagazine article written by Congressman Walter, claiming that "Mexico and Cuba now become the links of an underground railroad that carries Communist sympathizers from the U. S. to Moscow." When the teacher protested to Congressman James Roosevelt that she was about to lose her job because of the mention, Roosevelt asked for a check of the HUAC files and was told they revealed nothing against the Mexico City schoolteacher. She lost her job anyway.

In still another mistaken-identity case involving the HUAC files, a young Denver physician who had established a growing practice in a neighboring suburb, and his wife, were called to testify before the Committee and explain allegations in the Committee file that he had been a member of a Communist Party "cell" in Denver. He was able to prove that he had been in the East attending medical school during the period in question. But his practice dropped significantly after news of his appearance before the HUAC was publicized, and it took several years to rebuild.

The Committee's propensity for fingering "the wrong man" was shown also when two young people from New York and New Jersey were referred to as Communists by Congressman Walter during a HUAC investigation of American youth participation in alleged Communist-controlled worldwide youth congresses. Congressman Walter later admitted he was in error.

In 1961 the ACLU reviewed its files to compile some of the ways in which individual lives had been damaged:

· In Seattle, a member of the Molders' Union was called a Communist by a HUAC witness, but he himself was never called to testify. A woman kept calling his employer every day for weeks; he was finally fired.

· A Rhode Island housewife who refused to testify found her family socially ostracized; she was refused an active role in the state PTA in which she had formerly been an important participant, and her youngster was so affected that the family was forced to transfer him to another school.

· A successful Miami businessman-builder who relied on his Fifth Amendment privilege before HUAC, lost his business and finally had to leave Florida; he was forced to earn a living doing odd jobs and carpentry.

· A girl with a job as a potwasher was fired because her husband and father invoked the Fifth Amendment before the Committee. Her husband, a draftsman, lost his job, too. In a similar case in another city, a girl who worked for a county government division lost her job because her father declined to testify before the HUAC though she herself was not involved in the hearings.

· A fire-department captain who denied he was a member of the Communist Party at the time of his testimony but refused to discuss his past political activity, was dismissed from his post when he lacked one month and 10 days of 25 years' service and retirement benefits.

What Do You Think?

1. How would you define an "un-American activity"?
2. Should Communists who are American citizens be allowed to run for public office? Why or why not?
3. Should it be a crime to "advocate" the overthrow of the government of the United States? Explain.

4.   IS THERE TOO MUCH SNOOPING GOING ON? *

In his novel 1984, *George Orwell predicted the development of a totalitarian state where "Big Brother" would have total control over the lives of his subjects, even to the point of peering at them in the privacy of their homes through a device like a television set. Here Justice William O. Douglas of the United States Supreme Court expresses concern over the growing invasion of privacy by government and private employers as well as the danger of letting computers dominate our lives. How much information do you think the government or an employer is entitled to know about you? Might establishing such a file of information be a deterrent to dissent?*

The computer has taken its place alongside the A-Bomb to mark the second phenomenal revolution of this generation. An idea can now be transmitted around the world in one-seventh of a second. And so the recurring question is, what ideas will be disseminated? If they concern people, what data will go into the machine, how will people be evaluated, whose names will come out if the subversive button is pressed, the lazy button is pressed, the unreliable button is pressed, and the like?

If a centralized data center is established, as proposed, and all the contents of personnel files are poured into it, the privacy in this nation will be drastically diluted.

What is this privacy?

There is an area of privacy not expressly mentioned in the Constitution but within the penumbra [1] shaped by emanations [2] of its provisions— an area that has been held to be protected against state as well as federal action. *Griswold v. Connecticut,* 381 U. S. 479. In that case a Connecticut law made criminal the use of contraceptives and it was applied to a husband-wife relation. The court held that this law, as applied, was unconstitutional as it violated the right of privacy reflected in the penumbra of several provisions of the Bill of Rights.

The right to "belong," "the right to associate" is in the penumbra of the First Amendment which guarantees "Freedom of speech" and "Freedom of assembly." But it also extends where there is no "speech" or no "assembly." Otherwise those rights would suffer, especially freedom of speech, as joining a group, whether Communist or non-Communist, is a subtle though indirect method of expression.

---

* From William O. Douglas, "The Computerized Man," in a speech delivered at San Francisco State College, 1967.
[1] a partly lighted area
[2] a coming forth

The privacy of the individual has of course other roots in the Constitution. His religious beliefs are irrelevant when it comes to government employment. The human dignity of the person is involved in every case where the police through coercion or torture exact a confession.

The government investigator is bound by the Bill of Rights, as are Congressional Committees. Congress can investigate and legislate in the federal domain but in those processes it may not invade the individual's right of privacy nor abridge his liberty of speech, press, religion, or assembly. "What church do you belong to?" "Are you an atheist?" "What are your views on the United Nations?"—These and like inquiries are irrelevant to government. A man's beliefs are his own; he is the keeper of his conscience. Big Brother has no rightful concern with these matters.

Yet government agencies still exact information from employees concerning their religion, color, race, and nationality—all irrelevant to any government employment. Whites fear a quota system will be set up to assure Negroes a specific percentage of promotions whether qualified or not. Negroes fear these data will be used to deny them promotions. Whichever way the system may work, it sets in motion influences that have no relevancy to government employment.

All federal employees are asked, "Have you ever been arrested, taken into custody, held for investigation or questioning, or charged by any law enforcement authority?" Traffic violations and juvenile transgressions prior to age 16 are excepted. But false arrests are common; arrests for assertion of civil rights are frequent; many arrests never reach the test of judicial scrutiny. Yet all arrests go into the federal file.

Intra-personal family relationships have also been probed.
A Department of Labor questionnaire included the following:

I tell you like it is—it is rough out here, man—ain't like it use to be at home—those cats get you up tight—You ain't got your people —You are nothing.

You have to pick out one of five answers. The young man is arguing for (A) Family solidarity; (B) Defensive street group; (C) Solitary defensive activity; (D) Offensive street group; and (E) Group activity.

Which of the following is designed to affect the social relationships between racial and ethic groups: (A) Court decisions; (B) Mass demonstrations, 'The movement'; (C) Federal Government operation of installations; (D) Civil rights legislation; and (E) Executive decisions.

What was the average number of people living in your home during your childhood and your youth?

Have you ever felt some important person was bending over

backward to be fair to you, so you began to feel he or she was being too good to you?

Have you ever lived in a neighborhood with a large number of residents of the same minority group?

Just before your teens, how did you let off steam when you got angry; (A) By fighting; (B) By kicking or throwing something; (C) By cursing; (D) By talking it over with someone; (E) I didn't. I tried to hide my feelings.

Personal questions probe deeply:

Do you have any serious marital or domestic problems?

Are you, or have you been, a member of a trade union?

Is there anything in your past life that you would not want your wife to know?

Popular tests used in industry include: "Do you often feel just miserable?" "Is your sex life satisfactory?" "About how many people have you disliked (or hated very much)? (A) None, (B) One to three, (C) Four to ten, (D) Eleven to Fifty, (E) Over fifty."
One who hates four or more people is in trouble.
Another popular test calling for a true or false answer includes:

I believe I am being plotted against.

I dream frequently about things that are best kept to myself.

I am a special agent of God.

About half of the large corporations use personality tests.
School children, ministers, pilots, salesmen, executives, are often given these personality tests. . . .
If electronic methods are used to transmit the data to the data to the data center, what protection against "bugging" can there be?
Laws help and act as deterrents. But as we know, laws on wiretapping have had no appreciable effect on the use of that device. Making a crime out of the use of electronic devices to find out what a person's private life is like is one proposal. But since the police themselves are addicted to the practice, it is difficult to imagine them becoming effective law enforcement officials at that level. Laws directed against improper computer use may create a sense of security but they will afford no protection against Big Brother once everyone's ideology, reading habits, sex life, and various idiosyncracies get into the tape. After all, the information from the central data center travels on telephone wires and many people have access to them. Cryptography can afford some protection; but even it is not "foolproof."

Leakage of information into unauthorized hands is only a collateral matter. Why Big Brother should be allowed in the first place to put into a data bank personality and ideological data about anyone is the initial question. If we get a police state without a data center, the police state will be the first to create one. If we get a data center first we are well on our way to subordinating everyone to bureaucratic surveillance, to police surveillance, to political surveillance. Then we become serfs in the new feudalism that has overtaken us.

Those who are proposing the new data center are well-intentioned. They see much value in centralized data. But if traffic statistics, military statistics, census statistics, revenue statistics, Loyalty Security Board statistics, statistics on the politics and reading habits of the individual, his ideological bent, his youthful transgressions, his membership in a "subversive" organization that may have been nominal, fleeting, or thoughtless, and all the other facets of his life and his family's are retrievable if one only presses a button, what temptation there will be to use it! Our revenue statistics were confidential in the beginning; yet now they are available to the states and to numerous other federal agencies. The reasons for using collected and stored information increases in periods of mounting tensions or where political or popular pressures are great. The very existence of a pool of data on every facet of a man's life makes the temptation irresistible when a party or a people are out to destroy him. . . .

One's ideology, like one's religious beliefs or artistic tastes or reading habits, should be beyond the reach of legal process.

The dossiers [3] collected by government on people should never go into a computer system unless the items reported are as definitely objective as date and place of birth, sex, extent of education, and the like. Even the item "Were you ever arrested?" needs special protection unless a system for erasing "arrests" where the person was later vindicated is designed and unless "arrests" made in the guise say of "disorderly conduct" where the real charge was assertion of a First Amendment right are excluded. One person's appraisal of another should likewise never be fed into a computer, for that appraisal, though highly prejudiced, is quickly turned into a "fact" by the machine.

What Do You Think?

1.   Should wiretapping be allowed in certain cases, such as those involving national security?

---

[3] collections of documents giving information about a person

2.   Is it possible to "test" an individual's personality?
3.   If a person has a criminal record, should that be available to prospective employers?
4.   Is Justice Douglas a dissenter? Explain.

5.   DISSENT YES, VIOLENCE NO? *

The statement was once made that "freedom is never thought into existence . . . it is fought into existence." Discuss your reaction to this idea after reading Dr. Martin Luther King's argument for nonviolence. Is nonviolence a solution to the problem of dissent?

The experience in Montgomery [the bus boycott] did more to clarify my thinking on the question of nonviolence than all of the books that I had read. As the days unfolded I became more and more convinced of the power of nonviolence. Living through the actual experience of the protest, nonviolence became more than a method to which I gave intellectual assent; it became a commitment to a way of life. Many issues I had not cleared up intellectually concerning nonviolence were now solved in the sphere of practical action.

A few months ago I had the privilege of traveling to India. The trip had a great impact on me personally and left me even more convinced of the power of nonviolence. It was a marvelous thing to see the amazing results of a nonviolent struggle. India won her independence, but without violence on the part of Indians. The aftermath of hatred and bitterness that usually follows a violent campaign is found nowhere in India. Today a mutual friendship based on complete equality exists between the Indian and British people within the commonwealth.

I do not want to give the impression that nonviolence will work miracles overnight. Men are not easily moved from their mental ruts or purged of their prejudiced and irrational feelings. When the underprivileged demand freedom, the privileged first react with bitterness and resistance. Even when the demands are couched in nonviolent terms, the initial response is the same. I am sure that many of our white brothers in Montgomery and across the south are still bitter toward Negro leaders, even though these leaders sought to follow a way of love and nonviolence. So the nonviolent approach does not immediately change the heart of the oppressor. It first does something to the hearts and souls of those committed to it. It gives them new self-respect; it calls up resources of strength and courage that they did not know they had. Finally, it reaches the opponent and so stirs his conscience that reconciliation becomes a reality.

---

* Excerpted from Martin Luther King, "Pilgrimage to Nonviolence," reprinted by the Christian Century Foundation from the *Christian Century*, April 13, 1960.

1. Why did Dr. King think that nonviolent methods were essential to the cause of freedom? Would you agree? Why or why not?
2. Do most of the Negro people feel this way? What evidence can you offer to support your opinion?
3. Is nonviolence still an effective way to dissent? Explain.

6. BUILD A BLACK COMMUNITY? *

Would the biulding of a black community ease this aspect of today's dissent? This is what the longshoreman-philosopher Eric Hoffer suggests.

First, they tell you it's jobs; then they say it's lousy housing; then they say it's something else. What you have here is this: More than half the Negro population is 18 and under. They are juveniles. Secondly, you have a wide streak of juvenility in every Negro in the civil-rights movement. So you have juvenile delinquency on a national scale. Any time you think you are going to stop juvenile delinquency by giving them what they ask for, go ahead and give the Negro what he asks for and wait.

I'll start by admitting that all the Negro demands are just. But the fact remains that so long as the Negro does not demand much of himself, he won't get anywhere. No matter how much you give him, no matter how justified his demands, if he doesn't demand much of himself, it doesn't matter. Another thing is, the Negro is cutting himself off from his middle class. And if you have a minority that is losing its middle class, you have an awful mess. Without a middle class you cannot build a community. The Negro middle class must be bribed, coerced, anything, into reintegrating itself with the Negro masses in the building of a community.

1. Is the civil rights movement "juvenile" as the author suggests? Explain.
2. Have Negro militants lost the support of their own middle class?
3. Mr. Hoffer argues that a middle class is especially important

* Eric Hoffer, in a personal statement to interviewer.

if black people are to improve themselves. What does he mean? Would you agree or not? Explain.

4.   What does Mr. Hoffer mean by "community"? What other type of community might there be?

7.   THE RESPONSIBILITY OF THE REBEL *

In a speech at Brooklyn College shortly after a student strike in 1968, New York City Mayor John V. Lindsay expressed some hopes for the future. Do these hopes seem to be coming true?

Perhaps the falsehoods and inequities confronting this generation are not very different from those in existence two decades ago. The difference may be in your sensitivity to them. Certainly there is much in the world around us for the young to dissent from, to rebel against:

You have seen a declared segregationist assume the highest office of a state while Martin Luther King is confined to prison.

You have seen the Congress refuse funds to an emergency job program on the grounds of economy, in the same month that money was voted to revive the Subversive Activities Control Board.

You have seen the highest priority given to a supersonic airplane and pious handwringing devoted to the burning slums.

Each of you—as Americans and as students—must choose his response. The majority, perhaps, will remain basically apathetic and indifferent. They will follow the path of the mass of students in each decade before, those whose dreams and values have not gone beyond the bounds of personal economic and social success.

Others are choosing a different, even bizarre, course. In the case of the hippies, it is a flowery, melodious, and colorful life—a life that for some is dependent upon drugs and stimulants, and that for many is an unrealistic retreat from the problems of the world.

Another course is open to those who would constitute the "prophetic minority" of their generation. They are the activists—or perhaps more precisely, the protesters. They react to the world not by turning their backs upon it, but by facing it honestly—as it is.

The protesters are found in the picket line, at the teach-in, and at the mass rally. Like the hippies, they identify the hysteria, the artificiality, and the madness of much of the modern world. Unlike society's dropouts, they believe the world can be changed, and that they can be the progenitors. Certainly this country needs the reformer's zeal, for it is a nation:

---

* John V. Lindsay, "The Responsibility of the Rebel," *Class of 1968,* a Scholastic publication, 1968.

In which the natural beauty of our woods, mountains, and rivers is being vilified and destroyed. . . .

In which the affluence of the world's richest country is unshared by millions of Americans in the Appalachias and the Brownsvilles. . . .

In which our cities demand that those who would live in them must surrender the most ordinary expectations of comfort, grace, or even decency. . . .

In which the highest levels of government and business regularly are disgraced by cynical corruptions and betrayals of trust.

Those who would rebel against the values and conventions of our society have sound grounds—in logic and in conscience—for doing so. I should remind you, however, of the historic axiom that the rebel who overturns society's conventions assumes the obligation to construct new and better conventions in their place. It is by far the more difficult pursuit.

I believe that out of the recent turmoil we can establish here a close and constructive relationship between administrator and student that enhances both the human and intellectual aspects of the educational process. It will be a relationship, I hope, in which both the student body and the administration honor each other's right to talk and the corresponding duty to listen, and which eschews sporadic, destructive dissent.

The sophomore alienated from his school has much in common with the ghetto youth alienated from his city. Both suffer from an inability as individuals to influence the institutions that can better or worsen their lives.

This is the essence of powerlessness in modern society—the loss of will to try for constructive change. That absence of hope was apparent in every one of the American cities where trouble occurred last summer.

Yours is a generation that seems more and more to believe in the battle for change in American life. To channel that belief to the task of restoring responsive government to the cities of America remains, I believe, the highest item on this country's domestic agenda.

The course of our urban society is at one of the many crossroads of American life, and we're counting on you—the young, the ambitious, the educated—to decide the paths we shall follow. You are coming of age at a time when the old order is crumbling, and a new society is struggling to take shape. You are among the most privileged citizens of a rich and powerful nation, and that position should force upon you the obligation to use your gifts for the advancement of your country and the human condition.

I like to think that what has happened here over the past several days transcends the obvious, immediate causes, and that the energy, the drive, and the fight you have shown here will be directed toward more universal undertakings, those that will determine what kind of people we are, and what kind of lives we shall lead on this lonely planet.

I hope so. For in the words of Tennyson's Ulysses:
That which we are, we are—
Made weak by time and fate,
But strong in will
To strive, to see, to find, and not to yield—
'Tis not too late to seek a newer world.

What Do You Think?

1. Does the mayor echo the feelings of any other dissenters in this book?
2. Why is there a lack of dialogue between students and administrators? Does such a gap exist for the same reasons as that between teachers and administrators?

ACTIVITIES FOR INVOLVEMENT

1. Are most of the students in your school "conformists"? Why not find out? One way that sociologists study society is by the use of questionnaires, either written or oral. Plan a study of your student body in just such a way. Select a group of four or five students to draw up an "opinion poll " asking pertinent questions about topics that are of interest or concern to young people today, such as the sample below. Since a "yes" or "no" answer is often inadequate for questions of a controversial nature, it is suggested you give a wider choice to such questions by using the following method:

Check one:

1. With regard to school regulations on dress and personal grooming:
_____ the present regulations are satisfactory

_____ there should be no regulations

_____ the regulations should be stricter

The reason for the lines below each statement is to allow for further divergence or limitation of opinion. If, for instance, a student checked off the first statement in the above sample, he may want to add something such as this: "The regulations are ok, but the punishment, suspension from school, is too severe." Have the class tabulate the results, and write up the story for the school and local newspaper.

2. If there is a chapter of the American Civil Liberties Union in

your community, call them and request a guest speaker. This organization is a voluntary group devoted to the cause of protecting the civil liberties guaranteed in the Constitution and the Bill of Rights. The ACLU has provided legal defense for many cases such as those mentioned in the introduction to this booklet.

3.   Prepare a debate on the topic, Resolved: The draft is a legitimate use of Constitutional power. The magazine *Current* for December, 1967, has several selections giving background material on cases attempting to prove the draft unconstitutional.

4.   What rights are you denied because of age? The statement is often made that "If you are old enough to fight, you are old enough to vote." Have the class draw up a Bill of Rights for those under the age of 21.

5.   Review all the examples of dissent presented in this book. Poll a random sample of students in your school as to which they would be *most* likely to endorse. Then poll a random sample of adults in your community on the same question. Compare the sets of results. How would you account for the differences or similarities?

6.   Obtain a copy of the Bill of Rights. Without revealing the source, poll a random sample of students, teachers and community members as to which rights they would endorse. Tabulate your results. How would you explain your results?

7.   Hold a final classroom discussion on the topic "Voices of Dissent: Positive Good or Disruptive Evil?" Where do *you* stand on this question?

BIBLIOGRAPHY
For Further Study

Books

CLEAVER, ELDRIDGE · *Soul on Ice* · New York, N. Y.: McGraw-Hill Book Co., 1968.

DRAPER, HAL · *Berkeley: The New Student Revolt* · New York, N. Y.: Grove Press, 1965.

ERIKSON, ERIK H. · *Youth: Change and Challenge* · New York, N. Y.: Basic Books, Inc., 1963.

EKIRCH, ARTHUR A. (ed.), · *Voices in Dissent* · New York, N. Y.: The Citadel Press, 1964.

FORTAS, ABE · *Concerning Dissent and Civil Disobedience* · New York, N. Y.: Signet Broadside, 1968.

GOODMAN, PAUL · *Seeds of Liberation* · New York, N. Y.: George Braziller Inc., 1964.

HOWE, IRVING · *The Radical Papers* · Garden City, N. Y.: Anchor Books, 1966. (paperback)

JOSEPHSON, ERIC and MARY (eds.) · *Man Alone: Alienation in Modern Society* · New York, N. Y.: Dell Publishing Co., 1962. (paperback)

LYND, STAUGHTON, (ed.) · *Nonviolence in America: A Documentary History* · Indianapolis, Ind.: Bobbs-Merril Co., 1966.

MCWILLIAMS, CAREY · *Brothers Under the Skin* · New York, N. Y.: Little, Brown & Co., 1951.

MALCOLM X · *Autobiography of Malcolm X* · New York, N. Y.: Grove Press, 1966. (paperback)

MALLERY, DAVID · *Ferment on the Campus* · New York, N. Y.: Harper & Row, 1966.

MATSON, FLOYD W. · *Voices of Crisis* · New York, N. Y.: Odyssey Press, 1967. (paperback)

MULLER, HERBERT J. · *Freedom in the Ancient World* · New York, N. Y.: Harper & Brothers, 1961.

THAYER, GEORGE · *The Farther Shores of Politics* · New York, N. Y.: Simon and Schuster, 1967.

WEINBERG, ARTHUR and LILA (eds.) · *The Muckrakers* · New York, N. Y.: Simon and Schuster, 1961.

WESTIN, ALAN F. · *Freedom Now* · New York, N. Y.: Basic Books, Inc., 1964.

Articles

BINGHAM, CHARLES · "The First Amendment and the College Student," *Student,* September 1968.

CARPER, JEAN · "The Real Crime of Dr. Spock," *The Nation,* March 11, 1968.

COYNE, JOHN R. · "Crime on the Campus," *National Review,* October 8, 1968.

DAVIS, FRED · "Why All of Us May Be Hippies Someday," *Trans-action,* December 1967. (Note: the same issue contains two other articles on the hippie movement.)

HART, JEFFREY · "Violence in America," *National Review,* June 18, 1968.

HERBERG, WILL · "Alienation, Dissent and the Intellectual," *National Review,* July 30, 1968.

JENNINGS, FRANK G. · "The Savage Rage of Youth," *Saturday Review,* June 15, 1968.

KENISTON, KENNETH · "Young Radicals and the Fear of Power," *The Nation,* March 18, 1968.

KENNAN, GEORGE F. · "Rebels Without a Program," *The New York Times Magazine,* January 21, 1968.

LEAMER, LAWRENCE · "George Wallace/Dick Gregory—The Black and White of It," *Student,* September 1968.

LYND, STAUGHTON · "The New Left: On Defining War Crimes," *Current,* May 1968.

RIESMAN, DAVID · "Some Reservations About Black Power," *Trans-action,* November 1967.

ROSZAK, THEODORE · "Youth and the Great Refusal," *The Nation,* March 25, 1968 (2 parts, second part April 1, 1968).

SANDERS, FREDERICK · "Mr. Thoreau's Timebomb," *National Review,* June 4, 1968.

SWANSTON, DAVID · "The Meddlers at Berkeley," *The Nation,* February 5, 1968.

Films

Boston Tea Party (27 min; B/W; CBS "You Are There" Series) · Colonists' protest against taxation.

Death of Socrates (27 min; B/W; CBS "You Are There" Series) · Deals with the last hours of Socrates in 399 B.C.

Frederick Douglass (50 min; B/W; Profiles In Courage Series) · The story of the escaped slave who became orator, editor, diplomat, and leader in the abolitionist movement.

Ghandi (26 min; B/W; McGraw-Hill Biography Series) · The life of the man who led India to independence by the use of a unique weapon—nonviolence.

Harriet Tubman and the Underground Railroad (Parts I & II, 54 min; B/W; McGraw-Hill) · The story of the runaway slave who helped other slaves to gain their freedom.

History of the Negro in America (Three reels, 20 min each; B/W; McGraw-Hill) · These films follow the history of the Negro from the promise of equality set forth in the Declaration of Independence to the continued struggle for that equality in modern times.

Joseph McCarthy (26 min; B/W; McGraw-Hill Biography Series) · This film includes scenes from the famous Army-McCarthy hearings.

Sit-In (Two parts, 54 min; B/W; NBC "White Paper" production) · Contains interviews with people who were involved in the Nashville sit-in demonstrations, and an in-depth analysis of the situation.

Walk in My Shoes (Two parts, 54 min; B/W) · This film explores the world of the Negro American and listens to him as he speaks in many voices: the Black Muslims, the advocates of violence and nonviolence, and the whole diversity of views found in the Negro community.

The Women Get the Vote (27 min; B/W; CBS News 20th Century production) · The story of the struggle to secure voting rights for women.

Filmstrips

The Accomplished Generation (Guidance Associates, N. Y.) · Dramatic case histories show true individuality, social and political commitment, creative involvement among young people who are working to improve society.

The Alienated Generation (Guidance Associates, N. Y.) · Students meet hippies of Haight-Ashbury, learn why they are rebelling against society. Program emphasizes alternative ways of effecting social change.

Civil Disobedience (Guidance Associates, N. Y.) · Traces its history from Emerson and Thoreau, its relevance to civil rights, peace demonstrations. Philosophy of nonviolence. Produced in cooperation with the Associated Press.

Dare To Be Different (Guidance Associates, N. Y.) · Explores pressures to conform in our society, styles of nonconformity, suggests criteria for drawing the line betwen destructive and constructive reactions to group and social norms.

Dissent (The New York Times) · One of a series of filmstrips on social and political problems of the day.

Exploding the Myths of Prejudice (color; Human Relations Series; Warren Schloat Productions, Inc.) · Discusses the myths and misconceptions underlying racial prejudice, pointing out that prejudices are the learned results of an individual's social environment.

The Exploited Generation (Guidance Associates, N. Y.) · Probes the processes of commercial exploitation through mass media, particularly as focused on teenagers. Peer models speak out, encourage class debate.

Growing Up Black (color; Human Relations Series; Warren Schloat Productions, Inc.) · Reveals the realities of black childhood in our society.

Liberty Street—One Way? (Guidance Associates, N. Y.) · Shows precisely how *de facto* segregation prevents a Negro fireman from building the same good life for his family that his white friend enjoys.

Minorities Have Made America Great (Parts 1 and 2) (color; Human Relations Series; Warren Schloat Productions, Inc.) · Each filmstrip reveals the many problems faced by a particular minority group and recounts its contributions to American life. Part 1 includes Negroes, Jews, Germans, and Irish; Part 2 includes American Indians, Orientals, Puerto Ricans, and Mexican-Americans.

Rush Toward Freedom (color; Human Relations Series; Warren Schloat Productions, Inc.) · Five filmstrips show dramatic social revolution of the civil rights movement. Discusses violence, confrontation, direct action.

They Have Overcome (color; Human Relations Series; Warren Schloat Productions, Inc.) · Award-winning filmstrips documenting the achievements of five prominent Negroes in the face of enormous odds (Gordon Parks, Claude Brown, Dr. James Comer, Dr. Dorothy Brown, Charles Lloyd).